Bounce Back!

Resiliency Strategies Through Children's Literature

Mary Humphrey

Illustrations by Taia Morley and Megan Montague Cash

LIBRARIES UNLIMITED

U N L I M I T E D

A Member of the Greenwood Publishing Group

Westport, Connecticut • London

Library of Congress Cataloging-in-Publication Data

Humphrey, Mary.
   Bounce back! : resiliency strategies through children's literature / Mary Humphrey.
      p. cm.
   Includes bibliographical references and index.
   ISBN 978-1-59158-400-1 (alk. paper)
   1. Children's literature, American—Study and teaching (Elementary) 2. Resilience (Personality trait)—
Study and teaching (Elementary) 3. Moral education (Elementary) 4. Elementary school libraries—
Activity programs. 5. Resilience (Personality trait)—Juvenile literature—Bibliography. I. Title.
   PS490.H86   2008
   809'.89282—dc22   2007052931

British Library Cataloguing in Publication Data is available.

Library of Congress Catalog Card Number: 2007052931
ISBN: 978-1-59158-400-1

First published in 2008

Libraries Unlimited, 88 Post Road West, Westport, CT 06881
A Member of the Greenwood Publishing Group, Inc.
www.lu.com

Printed in the United States of America

The paper used in this book complies with the
Permanent Paper Standard issued by the National
Information Standards Organization (Z39.48–1984).

10 9 8 7 6 5 4 3 2 1

Bounce Back!

Dedicated to my mother,
who taught me love and resiliency

Contents

Introduction

Fostering resiliency skills has never been more important for the school and the community than it is now. Examining the state of families over the past five years indicates that large percentages of children come from "high-risk" families and face a diverse array of problems ranging from poverty (2% increase from 2000 to 2005), single-parent households (1% increase from 2000 to 2005; www.kidscount.org), poor health care, and the inherent risks of such environments. Yet even beyond these less than advantaged circumstances, children as a whole face the stress and strains of life in a complex world. More than ever, they need to be resilient, finding the way to right themselves, overcome adversity, and become healthy, happy, competent, and productive humans.

Research on resiliency is far-reaching and quite hopeful given that studies on resilience and youth development approaches indicate that such interventions can be highly successful. In fact, from the wealth of programs that support resilience-based prevention and education, certain indicators reveal that high-risk youth can be positively affected by such interventions. The long-range studies show the following results:

1. All youth, regardless of environment or background, show the capacity for resilience.

2. Certain strengths are associated with successful coping and learning.

3. Families, schools, and communities can play a large part in the development of these strengths.

4. Changing the course of a child's life begins with changing the attitudes and belief systems of the adults in families, schools, and communities. (From Bernard, 2004.)

Despite the lingering myths that seem to dictate a poor outcome for children who have experienced early childhood trauma (i.e., child care deficits, abuse, poverty), resiliency can be nurtured at any time with life-changing results. Popular misconceptions that resiliency is a trait—you either have it or not—must be overcome. In fact, resiliency is a normal part of human development; our innate capacity to thrive in spite of adversity is a built-in coping system. The plasticity of the human brain and its capacity to generate new cells and learning pathways has been proven in many recent studies. As stated by Daniel Goleman in his discussion of the *protean brain,* "the finding that the brain and nervous system generate new cells as learning and/or repeated experiences dictate has put the theme of plasticity at the front and center of neuroscience" (Goleman, 2003, p. 334).

In light of such research, it is well worth our effort as educators to support our students in their emotional and health development and contribute complementary programs within the school curriculum.

In this book the personal strengths associated with resiliency will be shown through some of the finest examples of characters and their actions in a wide variety of children's literature that will appeal to all ages, genders, and interest levels. An examination of these personal strengths will allow us to see how perfectly these characters cope, communicate, and problem solve, as they become the role models our students need. We will use the personal strengths of these book characters and organize their actions into five basic strategies for action:

1. Work on a Talent

2. Find a Champion

3. Look Within

4. Rescue Yourself

5. Help Others

As our students become familiar with these strategies, they will begin to personalize their own actions through discussion, critical thinking, and other activities related to the literature. In this way, we have introduced some of the finest examples of literature with the themes of resiliency to our classes and created a stage where the characters speak to the audience as they relate their own personal travails and show how they overcame the inherent obstacles to reach their goals. In turn, our students will speak to the characters as they draw insightful conclusions from their own personal history and transformation.

Before moving on to the lessons, let's examine the personal strengths inherent in resilient children to see exactly what we would expect from the characters in our books. These personal strengths are discussed in detail in the next chapter. For now, a listing of the personal strengths will suffice as we view them under our five basic "bounce back" strategies:

Work on a Talent	Find a Champion	Look Within	Rescue Yourself	Help Others
Personal Strengths Developed				
Mastery Competence	Communication Skills	Self-Awareness	Resourcefulness	Compassion
Positive Identity	Responsiveness	Insight	Self-Inquiry	Altruism
Discipline	Social Bonding	Intuition	Flexibility	Forgiveness
Self-Esteem		Autonomy	Sense of Meaning	Empathy
Confidence		Sense of Meaning		Caring
Perseverance		Humor/Irony		Humor

Working with These Lessons

The accompanying lessons work well with selected children's literature and are designed to promote resiliency skills and reinforce the language and concepts that define resiliency. Each selection taken from a range of children's picture books and chapter books that have wide appeal for both boys and girls is aligned with one or more "bounce back" strategies that specifically addresses resiliency. The five "bounce back" strategies are defined as follows.

1. Work on a Talent

Discovering one's own talents by working on what we love to do increases confidence and self-esteem and empowers one to realize that a skill in one area may positively transfer to other areas as well. The ability to persevere through difficulty is enhanced through the acquisition of special talent. Knowing that obstacles were overcome by learning a skill removes doubt and leads to new and easier achievements.

Personal Strengths Developed—Working on a talent develops positive identity. By perfecting a skill or talent, the child gains a true sense of purpose. By practicing the skill repeatedly, the child realizes that achievement in anything takes discipline, effort, and the willingness to persevere no matter what obstacles appear. Developing a talent requires resourcefulness and problem solving. Mastery of the talent builds self-esteem and confidence.

2. Find a Champion

Looking for someone who can help with the problem, either teacher, coach, mentor or another helper will give hope and the confidence to pursue it. The helper may offer encouragement, advice, or the one answer that bridges the problem to solution gap.

Personal Strengths Developed—Finding a champion requires communication skills. The child finds his voice as he attempts to locate that one person who may be able to help. To encourage the relationship with the helper, the child is developing skills that elicit positive responses through successful social interaction. The student/mentor relationship builds healthy, productive social bonds.

3. Look Within

The one avenue that is always available is the discovery that solutions often reside inside ourselves if only we look. Finding the good in a bad experience may lead to insights and solutions to present difficulties. Looking within allows creative and unique answers as well as limitless solutions to appear.

Personal Strengths Developed—Looking within creates insightful solutions and develops self-awareness. Insight includes natural intuition that alerts the child to danger. Insight allows the child to view her circumstances from a critical viewpoint and draw conclusions that may reframe his own personal situation. A child growing up in an abusive or alcoholic family may view himself as "different" and capable of becoming someone who can acquire healthy ways to find happiness outside the troubled family environment. Humor and a sense of irony may be developed as the child views his or her situation beyond the pain of the experience and into a positive future.

4. Rescue Yourself

Asking the right questions often leads to a self-made solution. Where can I get help? Who should I go to? What can I do? How do I do it? The solutions may not be far away but effort must be made in order to find the right answer.

Personal Strengths Developed—According to Wolin and Wolin (1993) self-inquiry is the personal strength that contributes most to resiliency. The ability to ask penetrating questions of oneself and uncover thought-provoking answers is a huge step in recovery and problem solution (Wolin & Wolin, 1993).

Flexibility is another strength created when immediate solutions do not appear. If the problem cannot be solved through one avenue, the child perceives that the possibility exists to change course. Getting unstuck by adapting a new course of action can be a highly effective route to resiliency. And finally, resourcefulness is the critical survival tool that enables the child to use his own strengths to cope and succeed.

5. Help Others

When things get tough, helping others may work as a "bounce back" strategy. Attention shifts when someone else's needs become more important than one's own. As awareness moves to another person, the importance of one's own problems lessens.

Personal Strengths Developed—Compassion, altruism, forgiveness, and a sense of humor are the personal strengths gained by reaching out to others. Through acts of kindness and love springs forth the compassionate spirit. Altruistic behavior comes from the child's ability to empathize with another and take positive steps toward the other's needs. The ability to focus on someone else's needs may involve forthright and encouraging communication, humor, or forgiveness.

The selected literature focuses on one strategy in each lesson; however, many times students and teachers will agree that the story's characters may employ more than one strategy in their problem-solving efforts. In that case, the primary strategy is emphasized, but students should be encouraged to identify as many of the strategies as they see fit. After all, the theme of all these stories is resiliency in one form or another; flexible, open-minded, and creative thinking should be encouraged and reinforced.

Each lesson contains a "Tool Box of Resiliency Skills." The Tool Box gives the students a graphic organizer for analyzing the character's main strengths and strategies. The Tool Box can be presented with blank boxes, allowing students to create answers for the characters, or it may be partially filled in as shown by the examples in the book.

Following is a sample of a student handout (from *Hanne's Quest*).

Hanne's Tool Box of Resiliency Skills

Hanne's Tools	Attributes	Student Responses
What she knows		
What she has		
What she can do		

After students gain familiarity with the Tool Box, they may design tool boxes for their own personal use. Follow-up activities may be to personalize problem solving and allow students to tell how they would address the difficulties of the characters in certain situations.

In the picture book selections, the teacher or librarian should use the pictures before and after each lesson to help students identify the strategies and relate which ones the characters in the story used. A lesson might begin with all the pictures displayed on the board or easel. Review the five strategies and what they mean to focus awareness on the various avenues to problem solving. After the lesson, allow students to pick the best picture that represents how the characters showed resiliency. More than one answer may be acceptable and encouraged.

For the chapter books directed to the intermediate elementary audience, the pictures may not be appropriate for this age group. The lessons for the chapter books have an additional feature known as "Story Breaks." The Story Breaks are possible stopping points where the teacher may wish to introduce or identify the resiliency strategy that is employed. Story Breaks are also used to note various literary elements, such as:

Point of View

Irony

Puns/humor

Vocabulary

Similes

Foreshadowing

Comprehension or discussion questions

At the end of each lesson, there may appear additional activities such as follow-up lessons, Web sites, or recommended reading. Additionally, reviews are provided to expand your knowledge of the book and its attributes. These lessons are designed to fit within the classroom curriculum and may be expanded or revised as needed.

References

Bernard, Bonnie. *Resiliency: What We Have Learned.* San Francisco: WestED, 2004.

Wolin, S., & Wolin, S. (1993). *The Resilient Self: How the Survivors of Troubled Families Rise above Adversity.* New York: Villard Books.

The Lessons

Picture Books

Hanne's Quest

Olivier Dunrea

Story Background: In this picture chapter book, set on an island off the coast of Scotland, Hanne, the smallest, quietest, and youngest hen, has been chosen to embark on a difficult quest. The little hen has learned that unless she can retrieve nine magical grains, find the Standing Stones, and face the formidable Sea God, all the speckled hens will lose their favorite nesting spots in the henhouse, and Mem Pocket, their kindly old lady friend and caretaker, will lose her farm. Hanne examines her fears and misgivings and wonders if she has the stuff to accomplish these tasks.

- Age appropriate for grades 1–5. Highly recommended for grades 2–4.
- Strategy that develops resiliency: **3—Look Within**

Character Study

Mem Pockets—the kind old woman who cares for the chickens

Daisy—her loyal dog

Hanne—the youngest and smallest black chicken in the henhouse

The chickens in the henhouse—Hanne's speckled friends who offer encouragement and promise for her quest

Old Pegotty—the wise, old gray and speckled hen who remembers the ancient predictions from hen lore

Pieter—a mole and Keeper of the Barrow

Keepers of the Stones (the Atecotti)—mystical creatures that can transform from stone to old and odd creatures, the Fates of mythical fame

The God of the Sea—an old sea turtle named Murdaugh

Master Oother—a boy who sells vegetables and oyster shells at the market

The Sly Fox—a man with a black bristling beard and a talent for stealing what does not belong to him

Introducing This Story to the Class

Although this story is newly created fantasy, it has many characteristics of a fairy tale. Students should review the elements of fairy tales so that they can be identified in this original story. The following fairy-tale elements should be noted and understood before the story begins:

The Quest—The quest means that someone must undergo a mission to secure something or accomplish a task. During this adventure, the quest taker must face tests. They will be difficult and will test this person's moral fortitude, courage, and resiliency.

The Magic Helper—Usually, but not always, the quest taker or seeker is aided by a magic helper. The helper may offer magical help or give good advice or encouragement. The relationship between the seeker and the magic helper must be trustworthy and respectful.

The Number Three—In the fantasy world, things often happen in threes—three wishes, three times, or three objects. Looking for the number three promotes attention to detail and gives the reader or listener a motivating reason to follow the story.

Story Breaks

Story breaks occur wherever the teacher needs to stop for discussion purposes. In this story, breaks should happen to help students recognize any of the elements of fairy tales, places where Hanne hesitates and appears to be losing her courage, and places where Hanne finds her resiliency and moves forward.

Not all story breaks need to occur for students to comprehend the essence of the tale. Teachers should use their own discretion and consider time and their students' attentional abilities before using the story break.

Story Break 1: Strategy 3—Look Within

Hanne is in a stealthy grip as the barrow-wight grabs her by the legs (p. 34). Hanne remembers that she has met the demands of the barrow-wight and commands him to leave her in peace. Looking within requires a "pause" or moment of reflection to assess the situation. Hanne succeeds because she has calmed herself and kept her wits about her.

Story Break 2: Strategy 3—Look Within

Hanne is able to proceed on her quest even though she is scared. She reviews her success in completing the first task and congratulates herself for not giving up (p. 37, "And I did not drop dead in my tracks.").

Story Break 3: Strategy 3—Look Within

Hanne would love to turn around and run home, but the soft voice in her head says, "Beware the false winds that blow" (p. 44). She pauses to think, and her mind clears to the truth of her circumstances.

Story Break 4: Strategy 3—Look Within

Hanne is overcome by the quickly rising tide, but again she looks within and remembers the advice of old Grainne, "Keep your wits about you" (p. 54). She is able to endure until she is rescued by the sea turtle.

Story Break 5: Strategy 3—Look Within

Hanne realizes she is too late to get on Oother's boat. From the bridge, she sees him pass below her. Knowing this is her only chance to save Mem's farm and return home, she jumps off the bridge and into Oother's boat (p. 66).

Hanne's Tool Box of Resiliency Skills

Hanne's Tools	Attributes	Possible Student Responses
What she knows	She was born at the full moon, and she might be chosen to lay three golden eggs.	She has been chosen for the quest because of her special ability.
What she has	She is willing to help Mem Pockets and save the farm. She has courage and pluck.	She wants to save the farm and the hens.
What she can do	She can try to find the nine grains and lay the golden eggs.	In spite of her fears, she will try to do the quest.

Using the Tool Box

The teacher may give students the tool box chart as a handout, or it may be re-created on the whiteboard for display. The attributes column may be left blank and filled in by students, or they may write or give their ideas in the third column. The chart should be designed to help students see how Hanne might use her resiliency skills to finish her quest.

Vocabulary

scaldy hens	the flock of specked hens
henwoodie	henhouse
clogs	wooden shoes suitable for farm life
babblers	small cubes of hard, brown sugar
satchel	bag
barrow	a mound of hill or rocks marking a grave
clamber	to climb or walk clumsily
wight	supernatural or unearthly being, the skeleton
barrow-wight	skeleton of the grave
conundrum	puzzle
pitch	black tar substance
lintel	headpiece over the door
skitte	to move quickly

Irony

Some students may be ready to identify irony as it appears in the characters of this story. The animals chosen to represent certain characteristics are known for opposite ones.

Hanne, the chicken, is brave and willing to go beyond the limits of her courage to succeed. The mole, Pieter, cannot see well, yet it is he who knows and finds the precise location of the rings.

The teacher should ask students what they know about chickens and moles to see whether these character traits line up with the known animals' characteristics. A comparison of these traits will show the meaning of the word "irony."

Comprehension Questions

Why was Hanne chosen to go on the quest?

How did Hanne succeed in acquiring the nine grains? (Name the three important aspects of this quest.)

Where does the number three appear in the story?

Of the five strategies, which one does Hanne use to overcome her fears? (Students may look at the poster to identify the strategy.)

Who are the magic helpers in the story? Name three and tell how they guided Hanne.

How does Mem Pockets prove that Hanne is her hen?

The Cameos

These are the small, round pictures that appear at the beginning of each chapter. The teacher should alert the students to the cameos so that predictions can be made about future events. For example, the cameo on page 21, Chapter Three, gives the reader a clue to the circumstances surrounding the barrow.

What the Reviewers Said

Booklist starred (February 1, 2006; Vol. 102, No. 11)

Gr. 2–4. Dunrea, the writer-illustrator of *Gossie* (2002) and other short picture books for the very young, now offers a chapter-book-length tale that is suitable for independent readers up to the middle grades and also fine for reading aloud to younger children. Near the village of Skara Bree, Mem Pockets lives with her faithful dog and her beloved speckled hens. When the old woman receives a bill for back taxes, she confides to the animals that she will lose the farm. The hens secretly confer and learn to their astonishment that one of their number, young Hanne, will be able to lay golden eggs if she has the courage and good fortune to complete a quest mentioned in an ancient rhyme. Quiet Hanne proves her mettle in a series of trials before returning to Mem Pockets' farm. The magical elements and the quest provide a familiar narrative structure for children moving from folklore to longer fantasy tales. The beginning of each chapter features a color cameo, a circular portion of the painting that will appear later in the chapter. Beautifully composed and often darkly atmospheric, the handsome full-page paintings rival, both in artistry and reproduction, those in the best picture books. This handsome, well-written book will find a rapt audience among children who prefer sturdy, homespun fairy tales to those of silk or gossamer.

School Library Journal (February 1, 2006)

Gr. 2–5. Dunrea clearly enjoys depicting barnyard fowl. In this lengthy, illustrated narrative, the protagonist is the youngest Scaldy in the henhouse. When she and her companions learn that their beloved owner is going to lose the farm, Old Pegotty tells them of an ancient secret: that a hen born at the darkest phase of the moon and [who] is capable of passing three trials might be chosen to lay three golden eggs. Only Hanne was born at this time, and the senior resident teaches her an ancient rhyme containing the clues she needs before she begins her arduous journey. After encounters with an otherworldly barrow-wight in the underground, the ancient power near the Standing Stones, and an enormous sea turtle in the "treacherous tides," she successfully completes her mission and all is well. The combination of folksy barnyard animals and the bumbling Mistress Pockets with the weighty quest plotline doesn't quite work. The rambling, predictable text, paired with one full-page gouache painting and cameo per chapter, also contributes to the sense that the book can't quite decide what it wants to be. Dunrea's hens and chickens are infused with charm; folk-art galleries would provide a better setting for his art than a chapter book. —Wendy Lukehart, Washington, DC, Public Library. Copyright 2006 Reed Business Information.

Student Handout

On the following page is a sample blank student handout. Teachers may create similar forms for all the books included using a word processing program.

Hanne's Tool Box of Resiliency Skills

Hanne's Tools	Attributes	Student Responses
What she knows		
What she has		
What she can do		

Rescue Yourself

Little Lost Bat

Sandra Markle
Illustrated by Alan Marks

Story Background: A Mexican free-tailed bat depends upon its mother for survival, but when this young bat finds that his mother has not returned from her daily hunt, he clings to the rocky ceiling of his cave hoping she will soon return. Based upon current research, this story is filled with scientific facts concerning bat habitats, hunting and survival skills, echolocation, and the ecosystem.

- Age appropriate for grades K–4. Highly recommended for grades 1–2.
- Strategy that develops resiliency: **4—Rescue Yourself**

Character Study

A baby bat
His mother
An owl
Another female bat

Teacher Preparation

Read the author's note on the last page to familiarize yourself with the fascinating facts about Mexican free-tailed bats.

Introducing This Story to the Class

Find out what the children know about bats. Collect as many facts as possible to ascertain students' knowledge of these fascinating creatures. Then explain that a species of bats known as the Mexican free-tailed bats lives in Bracken Cave near Austin, Texas. Explain that in one cave there is an area just for mothers and babies where mothers tend and feed their babies.

Location Through Sound and Smell—Tell how the mother bat finds her baby through both sound and smell. Imitate the bat sounds: "CH-CH-CH" for the mother bat and "Sh-Sh-Sh" for the baby bat. Explain the term "echolocation" and the fact that bats also locate each other through scent.

Predator and Prey—Review these two terms with students and explain the meaning of "ecosystem" if age appropriate.

Baby Bat's Tool Box of Resiliency Skills

Bat's Tools	Attributes	Student Responses
What he knows	He believes his mother will return.	
What he has	He has the strength and stamina to hang on to the cave ceiling.	
What he can do	He can continue to cry and search for his mother as the bat mothers return to the cave each night.	

Using the Tool Box

The teacher may give students the tool box chart as a handout, or it may be created on the whiteboard for display. The attributes column may be left blank and filled in by students, or they may write or give their ideas in the third column. The chart should be designed to help students see how the baby bat might use his resiliency skills to find his mother.

Vocabulary

echolocation   a process for locating a distant object by emitting sound waves reflected back to the emitter

adoption   to take a child of other parents as one's own

prey   an animal taken by a predator as food

predator   an animal that destroys or devours other animals, often for food

ecosystem   a community of living things sharing an environment

Comprehension Questions

How does a baby bat learn to recognize his mother? How does the mother find her baby?

What are the dangers within the bat cave?

What do you think may have happened to the baby bat's mother?

How did the baby bat find a new mother?

Review the Bounce Back Strategy Pictures

Have the children pick the picture that best illustrates which action baby bat chose (Rescue Yourself). Some children may pick Look Within or Find a Champion. These are also acceptable answers, and a discussion may ensue regarding the ways the little bat survived great dangers.

Additional Activities

Visit these Web sites dedicated to the survival of bats:

> • **Bat World:** www.batworld.org

Includes kids' games and information on how to adopt a bat

> • **Bat Conservation International**: www.batcon.org

A camera gives multiple views of a bat colony

What the Reviewers Said

Booklist **starred (June 1, 2006; Vol. 102, No. 19)**

Gr. 2–4. Through the story of one newborn bat that loses its mother, this beautiful picture book brings close the incredible facts about the more than 20 million Mexican free-tailed bats that live in a cave close to Austin, Texas. When the baby bat is born ("naked-pink and tiny as a peanut in its shell"), it crawls onto its mother, and, tucked beneath her wing, it nurses, "clinging to her fur / with tiny hooked claws." Every night the mother races out to gorge on insects, then returns to nurse her little baby. One night, she is killed by an owl, and the little bat waits and waits. Finally a new mother finds the baby and takes over the role of keeping it safe. The lucid free verse tells the elemental nature drama, and Marks' beautiful double-page watercolors with delicate ink details are equally effective at depicting the expansive blue sky and the tiny, furry brown baby, alone and then cuddled up safely at last. Back matter includes annotated resources, and amazing facts and numbers about bats that are as dramatic as the story. Children will want to go on from this to *Markle's Outside and Inside Bats* (2004) and *Markle and Marks' Mother's Journey* (2005).

Work on a Talent

Landed

Millie Lee
Illustrated by Yangsook Choi

Story Background: *Landed* offers a historical account of the difficulties of immigration in the nineteenth century. Entering the United States will be a challenge for Sun, who must pass an immigration test because of the 1882 Chinese Exclusion Act. His father has hired a tutor to coach the boy, but it will be up to Sun to remember everything accurately if he ever hopes to see his brothers again.

- Age appropriate for grades 2–5. Highly recommended for grades 3–4.
- Strategies that develop resiliency: **1—Work on a Talent; 2—Find a Champion**

Character Study

Sun Chor—a young boy, who will travel to America to be with his family

Mr. Chan—the tutor, who will help Sun prepare for his immigration test

BaBa—Sun's father, who will accompany him to America

Hop Jeong and Puy Gong—two boys who befriend Sun as he awaits his examination on Angel Island

Teacher Preparation

Read the author's note on the last page for essential background information.
Additional source: Angel Island Immigration Station Foundation Web Site: www.aiisf.org

Introducing This Story to the Class

Looking at the cover of the book, ask the children to discuss what might be difficult about coming to a new country. Explain that Sun was coming to America from China more than 100 years ago at a time when immigrants from China were not welcome. To become a resident Sun would be questioned by officials to prove that he was indeed the son of a merchant in San Francisco. He would need to remember everything about his home in China including directions from home to school. Sun's hope of seeing his family rested upon his ability to remember details accurately and confidently.

Ask students if they have a talent. Explain that Sun's talent is memorizing important details and being able to use a compass. With the students, pick out the picture in the book that best describes someone showing off his or her talent.

Sun's Tool Box of Resiliency Skills

Sun's Tools	Attributes	Student Responses
What he knows	Sun has dutifully learned all he needs to know to pass the test.	
What he has	He has knowledge from many practice sessions. He has his brother's compass.	
What he can do	Sun can continue to practice what he remembers about his home and family. He can use the compass to give himself a visual orientation of his former home and surroundings.	

Using the Tool Box

The teacher may give students the tool box chart as a handout, or it may be created on the whiteboard for display. The attributes column may be left blank and filled in by students, or they may write or give their ideas in the third column. The chart should be designed to help students see how Sun might use his resiliency skills to finish his quest.

Vocabulary

interrogation	an interview conducted by officials
abacus	Chinese tool for arithmetic calculations
compass	a device for determining directions
pedicabs	mode of transportation powered by a person on foot
Caucasian	of or relating to the white race
disembark	to remove to shore from a ship
an appeal	to take proceedings of a decision to a higher court
dormitory	a room for sleeping

Countries and Customs—Nineteenth Century

Specific items are mentioned in the book that note certain customs and culture for China and the United States. Have students fill in the chart that follows with equivalent items for each country.

Countries and Customs—Nineteenth Century

Item	Chinese	American
Transportation	Pedicab	Car or taxi
Food		Pineapple juice, fried potatoes, beef steaks, bacon, cookies, milk
Utensils	Chopsticks	
Calculator	Abacus	
Clothes		
Language	Chinese	English

From *Bounce Back!: Resiliency Strategies Through Children's Literature* by Mary Humphrey.
Westport, CT: Libraries Unlimited. Copyright © 2008.

Comprehension Questions

Why did Sun's father throw away the coaching book?

What is meant by a "paper son"? Why is the status of a paper son different from the status of Sun, who is joining his father, a man who has already established himself as a merchant in San Francisco?

Why did the officials wish to examine the compass that Sun was holding? What did they think he might be doing that was dishonest?

Additional Activities

Ask students how well they know their surroundings. At school or home, measure how many steps it would take to travel from one room to another.

Measuring Activities—School

How many steps to the cafeteria? Gym? Office?

Measuring Activities—Home

How many steps to your bedroom from the kitchen? The living room? The laundry room?

Make a Map of the Classroom

Sun has trouble with directions and uses the compass to find his orientation. Show how you would remember your surroundings with a map.

Label the walls east, west, north, south. Be sure to add the compass points to your drawing. Add other details to make the room memorable. Locate important classroom areas such as cubbies, teacher's desk, student desks, reading area, and so on.

What the Reviewers Said

Library Media Connection (November/December 2006)

Landed is based on a true story about the rigid restrictions Chinese immigrants faced because of the Chinese Exclusion Act of 1882. When his father tells Sun it is time for him to go to America where he will join his three brothers, twelve-year-old Sun prepares by studying for the difficult test he will have to take when he arrives on Angel Island. Sun enjoys the many new experiences on the voyage with his father, including strange new foods. Upon their arrival, Sun is separated from his father and sent to a dormitory. There he endures an embarrassing physical examination and the wait to undergo interrogation to prove that he is a true son. Sun passes and happily joins his father and three brothers in San Francisco. Each page of text is complemented by a full page, beautifully painted picture in soft tones of yellows and browns that portray the events of the story in a subdued yet moving way; both text and pictures convey the emotional control of Sun and his family. Readers and listeners will learn from the story and have much to discuss about Sun's experience. In addition, an author's note at the conclusion provides more information about Chinese immigration. Highly Recommended.—Susan Shaver, K–12 Library Media Specialist, Hemingford (Nebraska) Public Schools.

School Library Journal **(February 1, 2006)**

Gr. 3–6. Entering America from China will be difficult for 12-year-old Sun because of the 1882 Chinese Exclusion Act, even though he will be traveling with his father. He studies hard so that he can answer all of the questions the American officials will ask upon his arrival; he will be alone because his father, a returning merchant, will not have to be interrogated. When he arrives on Angel Island, where Asian immigrants are held for sometimes up to a year, he waits four weeks to be called. The only questions that he can't answer are about directions, and it seems that he might fail the test and be sent back to China. Finally, with the help of a compass, he passes the test. Based on the experiences of the author's father-in-law, the book recounts a story from a neglected and shameful era in United States history. An author's note gives readers more information about the history of Chinese immigration and suggests resources for further research. Choi's soft illustrations, reminiscent of those in Allen Say's *Grandfather's Journey* (Houghton, 1993), capture the spirit of the time with beautiful visual detail. This is a significant book; from it, students will learn much about this chapter in U.S. history.—Lee Bock, Glenbrook Elementary School, Pulaski, WI. Copyright 2006 Reed Business Information.

Highly Recommended Supplemental Titles for Strategy One—Work on a Talent

The Pot That Juan Built by Nancy Andrews-Goebel

The Boy on Fairfield Street: How Ted Geisel Grew Up to Become Dr. Seuss by Kathleen Krull

Frida by Jonah Winter

The Happiest Tree: A Yoga Story by Uma Krishnaswami

Look Within

The Librarian of Basra: A True Story from Iraq

Written and Illustrated by Jeanette Winter

Story Background: Alia Muhammad Baker is the librarian of Basra. Alia worries that the impending war in Iraq will endanger her precious books. Secretly, she devises a plan to save them.

- Age appropriate for grades 2–5. Highly recommended for grades 2–4.

- Strategy that develops resiliency: **3—Look Within**

Character Study

Alia—the librarian
Anis—the restaurant owner who is a friend of Alia's

Teacher Preparation

Find age-appropriate books on Iraq. Have a map or globe ready to introduce the setting of the story.

Introducing This Story to the Class

Ask what children know about war. What happens in war? How are people who live in a war-torn country affected?

Ask children to imagine what the effects of war in their town would be, without dwelling on loss of life and limb. Ask them to consider what buildings and places they think would be greatly missed if they were destroyed.

Have them estimate the number of books in their library. Obtain the library statistics from their school library to determine the number of books in the library. Ask what could be done to save the books in case of a war.

Find Iraq on the map or globe. Locate the city of Basra.

Have the children give their answers to these questions before reading the book. Accept a wide variety of answers without making any judgments. Ask them to remember their answers as they listen to the story unfold.

Remind the children to look at the five pictures of "Bounce Back" strategies. Ask them to predict which one Alia will use through her attempts to save the books.

Alia's Tool Box of Resiliency Skills

Alia's Tools	Attributes	Student Responses
What she knows	Alia knows that war is a possibility. She believes that the books may be destroyed. Many books are very old and valuable and cannot be replaced.	
What she has	Alia has the courage and tenacity to move the books herself. She is willing to take risks to save the books.	
What she can do	She can move some of the books to her home. She can ask friends and neighbors to help her.	

Using the Tool Box

The teacher may give students the tool box chart as a handout, or it may be created on the whiteboard for display. The attributes column may be left blank and filled in by students or they may write or give their ideas in the third column. The chart should be designed to help students see how Alia might use her resiliency skills to finish her quest.

Comprehension Questions

An important component of resiliency is the commitment to the task at hand. In what ways does Alia show that she will not give up, no matter what? See if children can identify at least three ways Alia avoids discouragement and continues to find a solution for saving the books.

Examples:

1. The governor refuses to grant permission to move the books, so Alia moves them herself.

2. In the midst of the bombing, Alia and her friends hide the books in Anis' restaurant.

3. After the bombing, Alia hires a truck to move the books to safety.

What risks did Alia take to save the books?

Why do you think the governor turned down her request to move the books?

Why was it important that Alia act quickly and do these things secretly?

Review the Bounce Back Strategy Pictures

Have the children pick the picture that best illustrates what action Alia chose (Look Within). Some children may pick Rescue Yourself or Find a Champion. These are also acceptable answers and a discussion may ensue regarding the ways Alia found help from others.

Additional Activities

Following the theme of finding peace within by doing something for others, the following three books offer additional activities and discussion.

If the World Were a Village: A Book about the World's People by David J. Smith

To create an understanding of global connection, make graphs representing some of the concepts from this book. Graphic representations of inequalities in money, possessions, electricity, and basic resources will help students understand their own roles and contributions in the global village.

Can You Say Peace? by Karen Katz

Read the book and say out loud each word meaning peace. Discuss the languages, countries, and cultures each word represents.

Peace One Day by Jeremy Gilley

Read the book about Jeremy's journey to convince the United Nations that the world needs one day dedicated to peace. Discuss the concept that it may take just one person to make a difference in the world. For example, if your students want to help Alia rebuild her book collection, they can contribute to a fund administered by the American Library Association. Make checks payable to ALA with "Basra Book Fund" on the memo line, and send them to International Relations Office, ALA, 50 E. Huron Street, Chicago, IL 60611. (For more information, contact the ALA's International Relations Department at 1 (800) 545-2433 x 3201.)

What the Reviewers Said

Booklist (December 1, 2004; Vol. 101, No. 7)

Gr. 3–5. On the heels of Winter's *September Roses* the author-illustrator isolates another true story of everyday heroism against a tragic backdrop. Books "are more precious than mountains of gold" to Basra librarian Alia Muhammad Baker. When "the beast of war" looms on the horizon, she and willing friends remove more than 30,000 volumes from the library and store them in their homes, preventing the collection's destruction when a bomb hits the building. As appropriate for her audience, Winter's bright, folk-art style does much to mute the horrific realities of war. The corresponding abstraction in the text, however, may give many readers pause. While an endnote explains that the "invasion of Iraq reached Basra on April 6, 2003," the nature of the crisis rocking Baker's homeland is left vague, and the U.S.'s role in the depicted events is never mentioned. At the same time, certain images—among them, silhouetted figures in robes fleeing from ominous tanks and jets—carry a pointed commentary that will require sensitivity when presenting this to children of deployed parents. Still, the librarian's quiet bravery serves as a point of entry into a freighted topic, and young readers will be glad to learn that a portion of the book's sales will go toward helping rebuild Basra's library.

Library Media Connection (August/September 2005)

Like other books by Jeanette Winter, this title was inspired by a true story. This colorful, bright picture book tells the story of Alia Muhammad Baker, the chief librarian in Basra, Iraq. It opens with a quote from the librarian: "In the Koran, the first thing God said to Muhammad was 'Read.'" Winter writes and illustrates a tale, which will be interesting to young readers and inspirational for adults. Alia knew the library's collection was not safe since war was coming. She hid most of the books, sneaking them over a wall into a restaurant with the help of friends. Thanks to her, although the library burned, the books were saved. The serious topic of war is made more accessible to students through the well-matched illustrations and text and ends with hope for peace and a new library. An author's note at the end of the book adds more information about Alia. The publisher is donating a portion of the book's sales to a fund to help rebuild Basra's library collection. Recommended.—Jackie Keith, Librarian, Riverbend High School, Spotsylvania, Virginia.

School Library Journal (January 1, 2005)

Gr. 2–4. When war seemed imminent, Alia Muhammad Baker, chief librarian of Basra's Central Library, was determined to protect the library's holdings. In spite of the government's refusal to help, she moved the books into a nearby restaurant only nine days before the library burned to the ground. When the fighting moved on, this courageous woman transferred the 30,000 volumes to her and her friends' homes to await peace and the rebuilding of a new library. In telling this story, first reported in the *New York Times* on July 27, 2003, by Shaila K. Dewan, Winter artfully achieves a fine balance between honestly describing the casualties of war and not making the story too frightening for young children. The text is spare and matter-of-fact. It is in the illustrations, executed in acrylic and ink in her signature style, that Winter suggests the impending horror. The artist uses color to evoke mood, moving from a yellow sky to orange, to deep maroon during the bombing, and then blues and pinks with doves flying aloft as the librarian hopes for a brighter future. Palm trees, architecture, dress, and Arabic writing on the flag convey a sense of place and culture. Although the invading country is never mentioned, this is an important story that puts a human face on the victims of war and demonstrates that a love of books and learning is a value that unites people everywhere.—Marianne Saccardi, Norwalk Community College, CT. Copyright 2004 Reed Business Information.

Find a Champion

Owen and Mzee: The True Story of a Remarkable Friendship

Told by Isabella Hatkoff, Craig Hatkoff, and Dr. Paula Kahumbu
Photographs by Peter Greste

Story Background: Owen, a young hippo, lost his mother in the tsunami that devastated Northeast Asia. In this remarkable and true story of resilience and persistence, Owen adopts Mzee, an Aldabra tortoise, as his new best friend.

- Age appropriate for grades K–6. Highly recommended for grades 3–5.
- Strategy that develops resiliency: **2—Find a Champion**

Character Study

Owen—a young hippo
Mzee (mm-ZAY)—130-year-old giant Aldabra tortoise

Teacher Preparation

Find a globe or map for location skills. Locate reference books appropriate for the study of hippos and tortoises.

Introducing This Story to the Class

On a globe or map, show the location of the Aldabra Islands, native home of Mzee, the tortoise, and also Kenya, where Haller Park can be found.

Discuss the tsunami of 2004. What is a tsunami, and how does it happen? How might Owen, the baby hippo, feel after being separated from his mother?

Find out what the students know about hippos and tortoises. In general, discuss their age differences and the amazing fact that they will become friends in spite of the fact that one is a mammal and the other a reptile.

Owen's Tool Box of Resiliency Skills

Owen's Tools	Attributes	Student Responses
What he knows	Before the tsunami, he was connected to his mother and the hippo community.	
What he has	He has the will to protect himself and the persistence to continue to request friendship from Mzee.	
What he can do	Owen can continue to nudge Mzee for protection and comfort.	

Using the Tool Box

The teacher may give students the tool box chart as a handout, or it may be created on the whiteboard for display. The attributes column may be left blank and filled in by students, or they may write or give their ideas in the third column. The chart should be designed to help students see how Owen might use his resiliency skills to find a friend.

Vocabulary

resilience	the ability to bounce back from a traumatic event
tsunami	an unusually large sea wave produced by a seaquake or underwater volcanic eruption
ecologist	a person who studies the relationships between organisms and their environment
mud wallow	a place to roll about or lie down in for refreshment
inseparable	incapable of being apart

Comprehension Questions

Ask the students what the following statement from the book means to them: "Our most important friends are sometimes those we least expected."

How did Owen and Mzee become friends?

In what ways did Mzee resist Owen's friendship?

How did Owen succeed through persistence to become friends with Mzee?

Review the Bounce Back Strategy Pictures

Have the children pick the picture that best illustrates what action Owen chose (Find a Champion). Some children may pick Rescue Yourself. This is also an acceptable answer, and a discussion may ensue regarding the ways Owen found Mzee as a friend.

Additional Activities

Visit the Owen and Mzee Web site to find additional activities and black-line handouts: www.owenandmzee.com/omweb/home.html

Visit Haller Park: www.lafargeecosystems.com/

One of the reasons that Owen and Mzee's friendship is so remarkable is the fact that they are such different animals. What attracted Owen to Mzee no one will ever know for certain, but their friendship remains true despite their obvious differences. Students can make lists of the similarities and differences between Owen and Mzee.

Similarities		Differences	
Owen	**Mzee**	**Owen**	**Mzee**
coloring and rounded shape		mammal	reptile
native to Africa		native to Kenya	native to Aldabra Islands
depend upon each other for friendship		young born alive	young hatch from eggs
both love water		may live to 40 years	may live to 200 years

What the Reviewers Said

Booklist (May 15, 2006; Vol. 102, No. 18)

Gr. 1–3. Originally published as an e-book, this photo-essay was conceived when Craig Hatkoff and his seven-year-old daughter encountered a newspaper article about a baby hippo orphaned by the 2005 Indonesian tsunami. Parent, child, and a naturalist they consulted are credited as coauthors. The story has a simple, direct appeal: the hippo is dramatically rescued and brought to a Kenyan nature preserve, where it forms a surprising bond with a giant tortoise. Inspirational language about "the power of courage, love, and the preciousness of life" clutters the powerful facts, and not all of the photos are equally crisp and closely cued to the text. But children will nonetheless embrace the incident's compelling anthropomorphic elements, thoughtfully framed by the authors, and will exclaim over the images of the winsome baby and its grizzled surrogate parent. Adults hoping to share the story with young readers may find this preferable to Jeanette Winter's picture book inspired by the same event, *Mama* (2006), which more starkly emphasizes the trauma of the tsunami itself.

School Library Journal (May 1, 2006)

K–Gr 5. When the six-year-old contributor to this book saw the photograph documenting the extraordinary friendship between a baby hippo (Owen) and a 130-year-old giant tortoise (Mzee), she persuaded her father to help tell their story. Originally an e-book, the hardcover version begins with images of the duo, whetting readers' appetite and providing reassurance as the potentially disturbing plot unfolds. After a scene depicting a pod of hippos near the Sabuki River in Kenya, the text describes the 600-pound baby's displacement and separation from the group during the 2004 tsunami. Children witness the challenging rescue and meet the knowledgeable staff at an animal sanctuary. From Owen's first approach for protection to Mzee's unexpected tolerance, the photographs, mostly by BBC photojournalist Greste, capture the pair eating, swimming, snuggling, and playing together. Their contentment and peace are palpable. Because it is sensitively structured, with careful choices about what is emphasized and illustrated, the situation does not overwhelm readers. The text and the back matter are brimming with information about the animals, their caregivers, and the locale. This touching story of the power of a surprising friendship to mitigate the experience of loss is full of heart and hope. A worthy complement is Ann Morris and Heidi Larson's glimpse at a human family's loss and recovery in *Tsunami: Helping Each Other* (Millbrook, 2005).—Wendy Lukehart, Washington, DC, Public Library. Copyright 2006 Reed Business Information.

Help Others

The Three Questions

Based on a Story by Leo Tolstoy
Written and Illustrated by Jon J. Muth

Story Background: Nickolai wants all the questions to life's dilemmas answered neatly and easily so that he will know exactly what to do all the time. In particular, he wants to know the answers to these questions:

When is the best time to do things?

Who is the most important one?

What is the right thing to do?

His friends—Sonya the heron, Gogol the monkey, and Pushkin the dog—try to help him discover the answers as they offer their own view, but finally it is Leo the turtle who is able to guide the boy on his quest for truth.

- Age appropriate for grades K–5. Highly recommended for grades 2–4.

- Strategy that develops resiliency: **5—Help Others**

Character Study

Nickolai—a young boy, who wants to find the answers to three important questions
Sonya—the heron, a friend
Gogol—the monkey, a friend
Pushkin—the dog, a friend
Leo—the turtle, a wise old friend
Panda
Panda's Child

Teacher Preparation

Based on Tolstoy's original story, also called "The Three Questions," about a tsar who asks the same three questions and discovers the answers when he unwittingly saves his enemy. Muth offers a gentler, simpler version about a boy whose quest leads him to the answers. Read the last page of the story to understand the author's reasons for rewriting this book as a children's story.

Introducing This Story to the Class

Write the three questions on the board before reading the book:

When is the best time to do things?

Who is the most important one?

What is the right thing to do?

Have the children give their answers to these questions before reading the book. Accept a wide variety of answers without making any judgments. Ask them to remember their answers as they listen to the story unfold.

Remind the children to look at the five pictures of "Bounce Back" strategies. Ask them to predict which one Nickolai will use through his exploration.

Nickolai's Tool Box of Resiliency Skills

Nickolai's Tools	Attributes	Student Responses
What he knows	Nickolai has a desire to do the right thing.	
What he has	Peace is a very special gift—one he can actually give to himself. Nickolai may not be aware he has this gift, but he can choose peace at any time. His ability to stay calm and peaceful will help him make the right decisions.	
What he can do	He can stay present with whatever is happening right now. He can recognize that the most important one is the one he is with. He can realize the most important thing to do is to do good for the one who is standing at his side.	

Using the Tool Box

The teacher may give students the tool box chart as a handout, or it may be created on the whiteboard for display. The attributes column may be left blank and filled in by students, or they may write or give their ideas in the third column. The chart should be designed to help students see how Nickolai might use his resiliency skills to finish his quest.

Vocabulary

noggin	head
splint	something used to hold an injured limb in place
deafening	a loud noise
drenching	soaking

Comprehension Questions

Finding personal peace is a large part of Nickolai's success in his quest. What are the peaceful solutions Nickolai discovered as he tried to find the answers to his questions?

Return to the three questions and review how Nickolai discovered the right answers. Place the book open to the page where Leo sums up the answers to the questions (kite and mountains picture).

"Remember then that there is only one important time, and that time is now."

Ask children to remember that staying in the present moment is always the best place to be. Worrying about what will happen in the future and what has happened in the past will not help in any situation.

"The most important one is the one you are with."

How did Nickolai realize that Leo needed help digging?

Why is helping the one you are with so important?

"And the most important thing is to do good for the one who is standing at your side."

Why is Nickolai unafraid to run out into the storm?

Further Questions for Discussion

What if you saved someone who was trying to harm you?

What questions would you ask the wise old turtle?

Which strategy did Nickolai use for his "Bounce Back" strategy?

Finding personal peace is a large part of Nickolai's success in his quest. What are the peaceful solutions Nickolai discovered as he tried to find the answers to his questions?

Review the Bounce Back Strategy Pictures

Have the children pick the picture that best illustrates what action Nickolai chose (Help Others). Some children may pick Look Within or Find a Champion. These are also acceptable answers, and a discussion may ensue regarding Leo the Turtle as the champion and teacher of Nickolai.

Additional Activities

Following the theme of finding peace within by doing something for others, the following three books offer additional activities and discussion.

Miss Rumphius by Barbara Cooney

Read the book and discuss ways you can make the world more beautiful. In addition to creating beauty, have children create lists of ideas for a commitment to saving and sustaining resources in the environment.

Something Beautiful by Sharon Dennis Wyeth

Take a walk around the school building, grounds, or neighborhood. What are ways students can improve these areas? What are class projects that may involve students in local environmental improvement?

This Land Is Your Land by Woody Guthrie

After reading or singing this story, compare the two full-page spreads of the before and after pages of the urban Depression-era scene (church, empty lot, and building).

Ask children to name all the differences between the two pictures. How was the same neighborhood changed and improved? Who do they imagine made the difference? Children? Adults? How did they do it?

What the Reviewers Said

School Library Journal (June 1, 2002)

Gr. 1–4. Young Nikolai questions Sonya, the heron; Gogol, the monkey; and Pushkin, the dog: "When is the best time to do things? Who is the most important one? What is the right thing to do?" Unsatisfied with their responses, he seeks answers from Leo, an old turtle living alone high in the mountains. He helps dig a garden and rescues a distressed panda and her cub in a storm. While the boy feels peace, he still doesn't have his answers, but Leo explains to Nikolai that if he hadn't stayed to dig, he wouldn't have heard the panda's cries for help. Therefore, at that moment, the important time was spent digging, the turtle was the most important one, and helping in the garden was the right thing. Later, saving the panda and her child were most important. So, now is the most important time, and the one you are with is most important, as is doing good for that one. Muth's languid watercolors, some sketchy and others fully developed, are vaguely Chinese in setting, and become less dramatic and more ethereal as the story moves toward its thematic statement. An author's note explains the derivation of the names and sources of the story, and gives a short statement about Tolstoy. This is a fanciful though not wholly convincing presentation of a Zenlike concept of what's truly important that would at the very least inspire discussion. —Susan Hepler, Burgundy Farm Country Day School, Alexandria, VA. Copyright 2002 Cahners Business Information.

The Lessons

Chapter Books

The Higher Power of Lucky

Susan Patron
Winner of the 2007 Newbery Award

Story Background: Lucky hopes to discover her higher power in order to save herself and her dog, H.M.S. Beagle, from almost certain abandonment. Living an isolated life on the outskirts of the Mojave Desert of California, Lucky believes that her guardian, Brigitte, will soon return to her beloved home in France. With a cast of quirky characters who are Lucky's friends and neighbors, she resolves to discover a way to change Brigitte's mind.

What the Class May Need to Know

The author references some resources that may be helpful to the story's meaning. The teacher may want to refer the class to the following resources:

The Tree of Life by Peter Sis (Farrar, Straus & Giroux, 2003)

Are You My Mother? Written and illustrated by P. D. Eastman (Random House, 1960)

The Web site for the International Guild of Knots: www.igkt.net

The prayer from the twelve-step meetings:

> *God grant me the serenity to accept the things I cannot change; courage to change the things I can, and the wisdom to know the difference.*

- Age appropriate for grades 3–6. Highly recommended for grades 4–5.

- Strategies that develop resiliency: **1—Work on a Talent; 3—Look Within; 4—Rescue Yourself; 5—Help Others**

Character Study

Lucky Trimble—a young girl with the gift of resourcefulness and many talents, including gathering insect specimens, dealing with scary animals, and surviving in the desert

Brigitte—a young woman who is Lucky's guardian and has cared for her since her mother's recent death

Miles—a five-year-old boy who visits Lucky every day; Miles is a tiresome pest with relentless requests for cookies and his favorite read aloud, *Are You My Mother?*

Lincoln—Lucky's friend whose mother named him Lincoln Clinton Carter Kennedy hoping that one day he will become the president; Lincoln has a fascination with knot tying

Introducing This Story to the Class

Lucky's town, Hard Pan, has a population of only forty-three people, and Lucky has one of the few paying jobs in the town—cleaning up after the various "anonymous" meetings (Smoker's Anonymous, Alcoholics Anonymous, Gambler's Anonymous, etc.) who meet regularly in the Found Object Wind Chime Museum and Visitor Center. Children will need to understand the importance of the anonymous meetings and the principles of the 12-step program to understand Lucky's fascination with discovering her own higher power.

Story Breaks

Story breaks occur wherever the teacher needs to stop for discussion purposes. In this story, breaks should happen to help students recognize any of the traits of resiliency. Story breaks also occur whenever Lucky uses one of her resiliency strategies (**1, Work on a Talent; 3, Look Within; 4, Rescue Yourself; 5, Help Others**).

Not all story breaks need to occur for students to comprehend the essence of resiliency. Teachers should use their own discretion and consider time and their students' attention abilities before using the story break.

Story Break 1: Strategy 3—Look Within (Chapter 3)

Lucky analyzes the good and bad traits of mothers by making two lists. It is this particular coping skill that allows Lucky the ability to think through her own situation and imagine the traits that mothers should have for the important task of child rearing. In her analysis of the bad versus the good, she is able to gain an insight into her own unique situation and comprehend that even from terrible mistakes, good things can and often do happen. Refer to the list on page 14.

Story Break 2: Strategy 1—Work on a Talent (Chapter 7)

Lucky's desire to be a famous scientist stems from the fact that something must be done to make Hard Pan a place where Brigitte will want to stay. Lucky figures that if she could attract visitors to the Found Object Wind Chime Museum and Visitor Center, it would be the first step on Lucky's way to becoming a world famous scientist. She devises a plan to attract visitors by collecting bugs and writing their stories on pieces of paper.

Through the enthusiastic endeavors of her primary focus—insects—Lucky has found a way to cope, and at the same time, it is her belief in herself and her talent for scientific exploration that releases her from despair. The possibility that Brigitte will leave becomes less likely as Lucky proceeds with a commitment to her plan.

Story Break 3: Strategy 5—Help Others (Chapter 8)

Brigitte is alarmed to discover that a snake has taken residence in the dryer. Lucky is undaunted by the snake and would prefer not to kill it. She uses her own resourcefulness to tape the dryer door shut and then stomps on the dryer. The hapless snake escapes through the dryer vent, never to be seen again. For discussion purposes, ask how Lucky's approach shows her problem-solving strategies and ability to deal with difficulties.

Story Break 4: Strategy 4—Rescue Yourself (Chapters 5 and 13)

Lucky has made a survival kit out of a backpack filled with items that may be useful if one is ever stuck or lost in the desert. In addition to the things she might want for survival (water and food), Lucky has planned to add the things her heart will need to stay brave. Putting together her survival kit not only provides the things she will need for protection in a harsh climate but also forms the fortitude of her conviction to help herself. Students might discuss Lucky's preparations and how her planning prepared her to deal with adversity.

Story Break 5: Strategy 5—Help Others (Chapters 18 and 20)

Lucky's resourcefulness pays off as she extracts the cholla burr from Mile's foot with Brigitte's parsley gadget, but it is a real test of her ability to step out of her own troubles when she saves Miles from further danger. Miles, intent on retreating from safety and expressing a desire to go home, is finally dissuaded when Lucky insists that he read to her his favorite book, *Are You My Mother?* From Lucky's insight and selfless behavior, she is able to cope with her own injury and Miles' need to find the comfort of home. Class discussion might revolve around the issue of why Lucky chose to bring the book along when so many other items were more essential.

Lucky's Tool Box of Resiliency Skills

Lucky's Tools	Her Attributes	Her Knowledge
What she knows	She likes exploring and is interested in many things.	She has an extensive knowledge of insects and desert animals.
What she has	She is brave and enjoys problem solving.	She rescues the snake from the dryer.
What she can do	She can try to find a way to convince Brigitte to stay in Hard Pan.	She can become a famous scientist and through her efforts create a new interest in the Found Object Wind Chime Museum and Visitor Center.

Using the Tool Box

The teacher may give students the tool box chart as a handout, or it may be created on the whiteboard for display. The attributes column may be left blank and filled in by students, or they may write or give their ideas in the third column. The chart should be designed to help students see how Lucky might use her resiliency skills to solve her problems.

Vocabulary

Some of the French words may need to be pronounced and discussed.

clafouti	French pancake-style pie with fruit
oh, la vache	Expression of dismay similar to "Holy Cow"
bisous	Kisses
ma puce	Affectionate term of endearment, literally meaning "flea"

Additional Classroom Activities

Create an Insect Museum (Chapter Seven)

Assign each student an insect to research for the Found Object Wind Chime Museum and Visitor Center. On a 3-by-5-inch card, write a story about the insect in a style similar to that Lucky used. The facts should be told in a way that creates interest in the insect and that relates their important characteristics. A clay model or picture may accompany the information card.

The Good versus Bad List (Refer to Chapter Three)

Create a chart (see sample on the next page) showing the good and bad characteristics of living in a town such as Hard Pan. Create another list showing the characteristics of your town or city. Draw from these lists conclusions about different types of living, their positives and negatives:

Rural versus urban

Desert versus forested, lake regions

Mountain versus low-lying, flat regions

Apartment versus house living

North versus south

East versus west

Good versus Bad List

Hard Pan		Your Town	
Good	Bad	Good	Bad

The Survival Backpack (Refer to Chapters Five and Thirteen)

What sort of things would you need to survive in the desert? Have students list survival items for their backpacks. Be sure the list includes some nonessential items for play and coping with boredom.

Comprehension Questions

What evidence does Lucky find that leads her to believe that Brigitte will be returning to France?

Why does Miles insist on reading *Are You My Mother?* over and over again?

How does Lucky prepare for survival in the desert?

What the Reviewers Said

Booklist (December 1, 2006; Vol. 103, No. 7)

Lucky, age 10, lives in tiny Hard Pan, California (population 43), with her dog and the young French woman who is her guardian. With a personality that may remind some readers of Ramona Quimby, Lucky, who is totally contemporary, teeters between bravado—gathering insect specimens, scaring away snakes from the laundry—and fear that her guardian will leave her to return to France. Looking for solace, Lucky eavesdrops on the various 12-step meetings held in Hard Pan (of which there are plenty), hoping to suss out a "higher power" that will see her through her difficulties. Her best friend, Lincoln, is a taciturn boy with a fixation for tying knots; another acquaintance, Miles, seems a tiresome pest until Lucky discovers a secret about his mother. Patron's plotting is as tight as her characters are endearing. Lucky is a true heroine, especially because she's not perfect: she does some cowardly things, but she takes pains to put them to rights.

School Library Journal (December 1, 2006)

Gr. 4–6. When Lucky's mother is electrocuted and dies after a storm, Lucky's absentee father calls his ex-wife, Brigitte, to fly over from France to take care of the child. Two years later, the 10-year-old worries that Brigitte is tired of being her guardian and of their life in Hard Pan (pop. 42 [sic]) in the middle of the California desert. While Lucky's best friend ties intricate knots and the little boy down the road cries for attention, she tries to get some control over her life by restocking her survival kit backpack and searching for her "Higher Power." This character-driven novel has an unusually complicated backstory, and a fair amount of exposition. Yet, its quirky cast and local color help to balance this fact, and the desert setting is fascinating. Lucky's tendency to jump to conclusions is frustrating, but her struggle to come to terms with her mother's death and with her new life ring true. Phelan's cover and line drawings are simple and evocative, a perfect complement to the text. Fans of novels by Deborah Wiles and Katherine Hannigan will be happy to meet Lucky.—Adrienne Furness, Webster Public Library, NY. Copyright 2006 Reed Business Information.

The Scarecrow and His Servant

Philip Pullman
Illustrated by Peter Bailey

Story Background: Two unlikely companions, a scarecrow and a young boy, Jack, embark on a curious adventure as master and servant. Little do they know that they are being pursued by a devious lawyer, Mr. Cercorelli, who would like to claim a mysterious document hidden in the layers of the Scarecrow's straw body.

- Age appropriate for grades 3–6. Highly recommended for grades 4–6.

- Strategy that develops resiliency: **2—Find a Champion**

In this book, Jack and the Scarecrow find champions in each other. A partnership formed to meet each others needs, Jack and the Scarecrow have skills and strengths that complement each other. When Jack is discouraged, the Scarecrow perks him up with a fresh outlook. When the Scarecrow is in trouble, Jack is ready to implement a new plan.

Character Study

The Scarecrow—He's looking for a brain—he loves adventure and excitement and sometimes he doesn't always think before acting

Jack—a boy, the Scarecrow's servant who is always hungry; Jack keeps his wits about him and often comes up with a plan to save his master, the Scarecrow

Mr. Cercorelli—the lawyer representing the Buffaloni family who seem to be taking over the entire valley

Granny Raven—the head bird who helps Jack and the Scarecrow defend the Scarecrow's claim to Spring Valley

The Buffaloni Family—brothers who have taken over Spring Valley and turned the area into a rat-poison factory, contaminating the waters and denying a healthy water supply to the residents of Spring Valley

Introducing This Story to the Class

To introduce the concept of resiliency, students need to see the two companions as complementary friends who give each other strength, hope, and comfort to succeed. When the scarecrow calls out for help after he is struck by lightning, Jack comes to his aid and accepts his offer to be his servant. The Scarecrow offers excitement and glory and Jack, having no other viable prospects, is happy to come along.

Story Breaks

Story breaks occur wherever the teacher needs to stop for discussion purposes. In this story, there are many opportunities to point out specific scenes that show Jack and the Scarecrow finding each other as means for rescuing themselves from dire circumstances. These scenes underscore the depth of their resiliency and provide the details of their uniquely complementary blend of skills.

Not all story breaks need to occur for students to comprehend the essence of the tale. Teachers should use their own discretion and consider time and their students' attention abilities before using the story break.

Story Break 1: Strategy 2—Find a Champion (Chapter 3, "A Story by the Fireside")

Identifying the strengths and weaknesses of the Scarecrow and Jack helps children see how perfectly these two characters dovetail their talents to find a solution to any dilemma. In this scene, the Scarecrow decides to hide in plain sight. Jack, seeing the futility of this plan, immediately launches into a story when the brigands arrive. As Jack's made-up ghost story progresses, the Scarecrow rises up off the floor at the story's climax, leaving the brigands frightened beyond belief. The plan succeeds by Jack's wit and the Scarecrow's flawless timing. Students can see how resilient these characters are even under the most death-defying circumstances.

Story Break 2: Strategy 2—Find a Champion (Chapter 8, "The Pride of the Regiment," and Chapter 9, "The Battle")

In this scene, Jack is indescribably hungry, and the Scarecrow is enamored with the idea of joining a regiment. To join, he must first pass an examination. After answering all the questions incorrectly, the Scarecrow is given the rank of captain, and the ensuing battle proceeds.

These scenes show the Scarecrow's bravery and heroism and Jack's indomitable loyalty. In the midst of a volley of cannon fire, the Scarecrow rescues a terrified robin and her eggs as Jack manages to barely hold the Scarecrow together. Once again, the pair's ability to render both their talents saves them under the bleakest of situations. Their combined qualities of bravery, loyalty, and compassion create a championship in the face of battle.

Story Break 3: Strategy 2—Find a Champion (Chapter 10, "Shipwreck")

Jack and the Scarecrow find themselves floating on a raft out at sea. As the Scarecrow relishes the excitement of an impending storm, it is Jack who uses his wits to keep things under control. Jack prevents the Scarecrow from opening his umbrella during the lightning storm, and the Scarecrow rescues Jack, who does not know how to swim. Once landed on a deserted island, the disconcerted and sobbing Jack is encouraged by the Scarecrow not to give up hope. It is in this scene that the resiliency of these two characters is thoroughly tested. It is only through their camaraderie that the two look for solutions and eventually discover a treasure chest. As further proof of their teamwork, the Scarecrow digs a well for water, and Jack figures out how to purify it. To relieve Jack's brutal hunger, the Scarecrow offers some of his turnip head for supper. This final bit of humor shows the resilient pair at their best in both generosity and spirit.

Story Break 4: Strategy 2—Find a Champion
(Chapter 13, "The Assizes")

Jack and the Scarecrow stumble into town just in time to face the court, the Assizes, who will decide the rightful ownership of Spring Valley. During the trial, it is Jack at his best combined with the Scarecrow's determination and confidence that wins the Scarecrow's claim to the land. With Jack's wit and charm and the Scarecrow's optimism and humor, the pair succeed in convincing the jury of the corruption of the Buffaloni family and that their claim to Spring Valley is legitimate. In this final test of their resiliency, Jack continues on despite the fact that he cannot read the document that holds the key to their ultimate victory. The Scarecrow resolutely claims he has an inner conviction even against the judge's claims of fraud and deception. In the end, the pair is saved by Granny Raven and her surprise witnesses, but it is really their brilliant strategy to persevere that ensures this positive outcome.

The Scarecrow and Jack's Tool Box of Resiliency Skills

The Scarecrow's Tools		Jack's Tools	
Attributes: **Courteous, brave, honorable, kind, and lucky**		**Attributes:** **Loyal, cautious, wise, and compassionate**	
What he knows	He knows he is the true owner of Spring Valley. He has an inner conviction that this is so.	**What he knows**	He knows he is loyal to the Scarecrow and that his role as servant is important.
What he has	He has an indefatigable positive attitude.	**What he has**	He is clever and thinks clearly and quickly.
What he can do	He can continue on even in the most adverse circumstances.	**What he can do**	He will do anything to help the Scarecrow.

Using the Tool Box

Use the chart provided to brainstorm qualities and attributes associated with resiliency.

Vocabulary

brigand	soldier who plunders
subtle	delicate, elusive, difficult to perceive
disconsolately	cheerlessly, dejectedly
consuming	engrossing
blunderbuss	a muzzle-loading firearm with a short barrel
caterwauling	harsh crying
fraud	trickery, deceit
ninny	a fool, simpleton
panache	flamboyance in style or fashion
ford	to cross a shallow part of water by wading
farrier	a person who shoes horses
gallant	courteous
shako	a stiff military hat with a plume

Similes

Gaping like a pair of flytraps (p. 128)
Heavy drops hurtled down as fast as bullets (p. 132)
Bobbing up and down like a chicken (p. 186)

Irony

Some students may be ready to identify irony as it appears in the characters of this story. The most obvious way to show irony is through the relationship between Jack and his master, the Scarecrow. Jack, wise beyond his years, advises and rescues the Scarecrow from innumerable scrapes; the Scarecrow, who is supposed to be in charge, constantly provokes risk and danger, which often prove fortuitous for the lucky pair.

Example: The Scarecrow answers all the questions wrong on his examination for the military while Jack worries about the next meal. The Scarecrow is immediately promoted to the rank of captain. Jack secures a delicious meal from the cook.

Puns and Humor

The story abounds with puns and nonsensical humor that children will love. Word play and double meanings in certain phrases will delight youngsters and add new meaning to the passages. The teacher should use the handout beginning on the next page to identify phrases and sentences with double meanings.

Twice as Funny

Phillip Pullman, the author of *The Scarecrow and His Servant,* uses puns to give the story a funny, nonsensical twist. A pun is a word or phrase that suggests two or more meanings in a humorous way. Identify the highlighted word below. From the context of the story, guess the second meaning of the word. Check the dictionary to find more than one meaning.

Chapter Four—The Scarecrow loses his rake handle arm.

"I've been disarmed!" the Scarecrow said, shocked. (p. 37)

Disarmed—to make harmless

Meaning 1	Meaning 2

Chapter Five—The goats nibble at the Scarecrow's clothes.

"They were taking a consuming interest in you, master," said Jack. (p. 61)

Consuming—deeply felt, engrossing

Meaning 1	Meaning 2

Chapter Six—The Scarecrow discovers that his broom is already engaged.

"She's already engaged!" the Scarecrow howled. "She's going to marry a rake!" (p. 79)

Rake—A lawn implement with prongs for gathering leaves

Meaning 1	Meaning 2

Chapter Sixteen—The broomstick is transplanted into the Scarecrow's back to save his life.

When the two of them found themselves united, their happiness was complete. (p. 227)

United—made one, combined

Meaning 1	Meaning 2

Chapter Sixteen—the broomstick has been abandoned and passed around.

She had been passed hand to hand. (p. 227)

Hand to hand—involving physical contact

Meaning 1	Meaning 2

Comprehension Questions

What qualities make the friendship between the Scarecrow and Jack endurable and successful?

What are Jack's fears when the Scarecrow boldly wants to join the regiment?

Why is the Scarecrow afraid of birds?

What have the Buffaloni family been doing to the waters of Spring Valley?

What the Reviewers Said

Library Media Connection (February 2006)

After being struck by lightning, the scarecrow in old Mr. Pandolfo's field comes to life. Young Jack is taking shelter in a nearby barn and, hearing the scarecrow's cries for help, Jack removes the scarecrow from the pole he's been hanging on. Lord Scarecrow, as he is later known, offers Jack a job as his servant, and they start off on their hilarious adventures. All along the way they stay one step ahead of Mr. Cercorelli, a lawyer working for the dastardly Buffaloni family, which has set up a poison factory in Spring Valley and dried up all sources of water in the area. With the help of Granny Raven, Jack and Lord Scarecrow meet up with the Buffalonis and their lawyers in court to prove that Lord Scarecrow is the rightful owner of Spring Valley. Disaster nearly strikes when the Buffalonis pour termites, woodworms, and deathwatch beetles down Lord Scarecrow's neck, which nearly results in his death. After a complete transplant of stuffing and a new backbone made from a broom handle, Lord Scarecrow is restored to his former good health, and like all good fairy tales, everyone lives happily ever after. This book will appeal to youngsters who like adventure stories with a healthy dose of humor thrown in. Recommended.—Ann M. G. Gray, Library Media Specialist, Pittsburg (New Hampshire) School.

The Miraculous Journey of Edward Tulane

Kate DiCamillo

Story Background: Edward, a much-loved rabbit, is made almost entirely of china. Although his young owner, Abilene, adores him, Edward rarely listens to her and is mostly concerned with his own appearance and prestige as the beloved toy. This remains the case until Abilene and Edward embark on a voyage on the *Queen Mary*. Edward is tossed overboard, and thus begins his miraculous journey of discovery, hardship, and triumph.

- Age appropriate for grades 2–6. Highly recommended for grades 3–5.
- Strategies that develop resiliency: **3—Look Within; 4—Rescue Yourself**

Character Study

Abilene—a young girl who loves Edward

Edward—the mostly china rabbit enamored with his own image

Pellegrina—Abilene's grandmother

Lawrence, Nellie, and Lolly—the fisherman and his family

Bull and his dog, Lucy—a homeless man and his pet dog

Bryce and Sarah Ruth—a poor boy and his sick younger sister

Introducing This Story to the Class

Discuss with the children their favorite stuffed toys or dolls. Ask if anyone ever imagines this favorite doll or stuffed animal as having a personality. What would it be like? What would the doll or animal say or do? Building on their relationships with their own toys, introduce Edward as a china rabbit so elegant and regal that he feels no interest in anything but his own beautiful appearance. Show the picture in Chapter Two and discuss how Abilene feels about Edward. Do they appear to share the same feelings. Why or why not?

Story Breaks

Story breaks occur wherever the teacher needs to stop for discussion purposes. In this story, breaks should happen to help students recognize any of the elements of resiliency that suggest that Edward may be beginning his journey of transformation. Story breaks will also occur whenever Edward uses one of his resiliency strategies or when a change occurs in his incredible transformation.

Not all story breaks need to occur for students to comprehend the essence of the tale. Teachers should use their own discretion and consider time and their students' attention abilities before using the story break.

Story Break 1: Edward's Character (Chapter 2)

In the incident with the maid, the reader clearly understands certain traits of Edward's. He is not the least bit affected, even briefly, by being separated from Abilene. He is merely annoyed by being humiliated (the maid refers to him as "a bunny") and annoyed by the way he is treated. Children should identify Edward's feelings here and begin to understand his personality.

Story Break 2: Foreshadowing of Edward's Journey (Chapters 3 and 4)

How does Pellegrina's story pertain to Edward? When Pellegrina says that the witch is disappointed in the princess, to whom is she referring? Does Edward appear to get the point of the story? Why or why not?

Story Break 3: Strategy 3—Look Within (Chapters 6 and 7)

At the end of Chapter Six, Edward experiences real emotion for the first time. Lying face down in the muck of the ocean, Edward is afraid. It is fear of the unknown that finally causes Edward to look within and ponder his fate. Through the hours, days, weeks, and months in solitude, Edward begins to examine Pellegrina's princess story. Again, refer the students to the princess story and its meaning for Edward.

When Edward is rescued by the fisherman, he feels the sun and wind on his face and ears. For the first time, he experiences the joy of being alive. How has Edward changed since the beginning of the story?

Story Break 4: Strategy 3—Look Within (Chapters 9–14)

In these chapters the reader begins to notice subtle changes in Edward and his relationships with the various people who acquire him. No longer do we see the self-centered Edward who thinks only of lovely clothes and his appearance, but now there is a new Edward who listens and appears to respond to the people in his life. Have the students list the ways in which Edward is responsive and curious (Example: Edward listens to Nellie's stories as if his life depended on them, p. 69). Have students notice how Edward is willing to be involved in other's dilemmas (Example: His desire to rescue Lucy, p. 105).

Story Break 5: Strategy 4—Rescue Yourself (Chapters 17–20)

The reader can see that Edward now has feelings and can care about and even love the people in his family. His love for Sarah Ruth is revealed after he can no longer see her ("He ached for Sarah Ruth. He wanted to hold her," p. 148). Edward's change is complete when he finally recognizes Pellegrina in the streets and pleads for help. It is his action, a request for help, that shows how Edward has been transformed from the self-centered, conceited rabbit to a mature, humble, and heartbroken soul.

Story Break 6: Irony (Chapter 25)

Introduce the concept of irony through Edward's opinion of the dolls (p. 181). As students discover the meaning of the word "irony," have them notice how the very traits displayed by the dolls (annoying, self-centered, twittery, and vain) are the same traits Edward once considered faultless in himself.

Story Break 7: Strategy 4—Rescue Yourself (Chapters 26 and 27)

Edward has nearly given up hope that he can ever love again until he meets the antique doll next to him on the shelf. It is only in a brief instant that his heart begins to open and create the hope he believed he had lost forever.

It is Edward's constant repetition of the words "Someone will come for you" that ensures his own rescue. Years pass, but Edward never gives up hope—the key to resiliency. At last the little girl appears who wants him, and the answer to Edward's most precious request is finally fulfilled.

Edward's Tool Box of Resiliency Skills

Edward's Tools	His Shortcomings (Edward, Chapters 1–6)	What he learns (Edward, Chapters 7–27)
What he knows	He is an attractive china rabbit with a gold watch and furry ears.	
What he has	He has a perfect china body, beautiful clothes, and a gold watch.	
What he can do	He cannot change unless his circumstances cause him to change.	

Using the Tool Box

The teacher may give students the tool box chart as a handout, or it may be created on the whiteboard for display. The shortcomings column may be left blank and filled in by students, or they may write or give their ideas in the third column as they see how Edward changes. The chart should be designed to help students see how Edward transforms and becomes more resilient as he opens to others.

Vocabulary

ennui (p. 5)
derogatory (p. 16)
cavalierly (p. 19)
ferocity (p. 55)
umbrage (p. 58)
vain (p. 181)
contrarian (p. 184)

Comprehension Questions

Chapters 1–4

Why does Pellegrina tell Edward and Abilene the story of the princess who is turned into a warthog?

Why does Pellegrina tell Edward that she is disappointed in him?

Why does Edward not understand the story of the princess?

Who is able to express love? Edward? Abilene?

Chapter 27

How does Abilene recognize Edward?

How do we know how Edward feels when he sees Abilene?

Who is Maggie and what is her relationship to Abilene?

How did Edward find his way home again?

What the Reviewers Said

- **Boston Globe-Horn Book Awards Winner, Fiction Category**

- **Quills Award Nominee**

"Kate DiCamillo gives us a fragile and wonderfully human anti-hero, and in this book she delivers a quiet, meaningful, and memorable story with all the markings of a future classic and wonderful sparks of Kate's signature wit." —Alison Morris, Children's Book Buyer, Wellesley Booksmith, Wellesley, MA

"This charming book is destined to be read aloud, shared, and savored by young and old alike. It has an old-fashioned quality and the appearance of a classic, and belongs in every child's library." —Pat Scales, Director of Library Services, South Carolina Governor's School of the Arts, Greenville, SC

"Edward Tulane does go on a miraculous journey, but the real miracle is how he is changed. From the bottom of the sea to a dump and beyond, this once glorious and much-loved china rabbit captured my attention immediately and took me with him on his amazing travels. With him I felt elegant, broken, frightened, hopeful, lonely, and ultimately happy. I was sad each time

Edward lost someone and moved by what he learned about caring and love. I want to read this enchanting tale out loud to someone sitting on my lap, and together we will predict what the next adventure will be as we look at the charming pictures that introduce each chapter. This beautiful treasure, with the creativity and artistry of Kate DiCamillo and illustrator Bagram Ibatoulline, is a story for readers of all ages, who will be reminded about what it means to be human."—Connie S. Zitlow, Professor, Ohio Wesleyan University; Editor of Lost Masterworks of Young Adult Literature; Past President of the Assembly on Literature for Adolescents

"The melody and rhythm of life's lessons about friendship and love are captured in this timeless story by Kate DiCamillo and illustrated by Bagram Ibatoulline, whose artwork is incredible. I think we have a new classic." —Joci Tilsen, Valley Bookseller, Stillwater, MN

"This tender story, with truly lovely art, will resonate with all of Kate DiCamillo's fans." —Margaret Brennan Neville, The King's English Bookshop, Salt Lake City, UT

"Exquisite language, inventive plot twists, and memorable characters."—*Publishers Weekly* (boxed signature review)

"Somewhere between fairy tale and fable, DiCamillo spins the tale of Edward, transformed by the lives he touches. The reader will be transformed too."—*Kirkus* (starred review)

"The story soars because of DiCamillo's lyrical use of language and her understanding of universal yearnings. This will be a pleasure to read aloud."—*Booklist* (starred review)

"Perhaps no other current American children's book writer has appeared on the scene so quickly or so brightly as Kate DiCamillo. . . . DiCamillo's latest novel, The Miraculous Journey of Edward Tulane, may well be her best. . . . One reading is hardly enough to savor the rich philosophical nuances of DiCamillo's story. I think I will go read it again right now."—*New York Times Book Review*

School Library Journal (February 1, 2006)

Gr. 3–6. This achingly beautiful story shows a true master of writing at her very best. Edward Tulane is an exceedingly vain, cold-hearted china rabbit owned by 10-year-old Abilene Tulane, who dearly loves him. Her grandmother relates a fairy tale about a princess who never felt love; she then whispers to Edward that he disappoints her. His path to redemption begins when he falls overboard during the family's ocean journey. Sinking to the bottom of the sea where he will spend 297 days, Edward feels his first emotion-fear. Caught in a fisherman's net, he lives with the old man and his wife and begins to care about his humans. Then their adult daughter takes him to the dump, where a dog and a hobo find him. They ride the rails together until Edward is cruelly separated from them. His heart is truly broken when his next owner, four-year-old Sarah Ruth, dies. He recalls Abilene's grandmother with a new sense of humility, wishing she knew that he has learned to love. When his head is shattered by an angry man, Edward wants to join Sarah Ruth but those he has loved convince him to live. Repaired by a doll store owner, he closes his heart to love, as it is too painful, until a wise doll tells him that he must open his heart for someone to love him. This superb book is beautifully written in spare yet stirring language. The tender look at the changes from arrogance to grateful loving is perfectly delineated. Ibatoulline's lovely sepia-toned gouache illustrations and beautifully rendered color plates are exquisite. An ever-so-marvelous tale.—B. Allison Gray, John Jermain Library, Sag Harbor, NY. Copyright 2006 Reed Business Information.

Project Mulberry

Linda Sue Park

Story Background: Julia and Patrick want to do an original and creative animal activity for the Wiggle Club's annual animal husbandry project, but when Patrick supports the idea of growing silkworms, Julia tries to sabotage their work because of her reluctance to associate with anything remotely Korean, her family background. As the two struggle to raise the delicate creatures, Julia begins to realize the importance of her ancestry as the project unfolds with an unpredictable and irresistible turn of events.

- Age appropriate for grades 4–8. Highly recommended for grades 4–6.

- Strategies that develop resiliency: **1—Work on a Talent; 4—Rescue Yourself**

Character Study

Julia—a Korean-American seventh-grade girl who loves spending her time on creative projects

Patrick—Julia's best friend who is creative, intelligent, and insightful

Julia's mom—born in Korea, Julia's mom has adjusted to most things American but still carries some issues with racial equity

Julia's dad—Julia's dad was also born in Korea; he is fairly open-minded, positive, and well adjusted to life in a new country

Mr. Dixon—an elderly African American man who provides Julia and Patrick with the mulberry leaves they will need for their project

Mr. Maxwell—the project leader of the Wiggle Club

Kenny—Julia's annoying younger brother; according to Julia, he is also known as "snotbrain"

Introducing This Story to the Class

Discuss with the children what it might be like if you were the first generation in your family to be an American. What would it be like to come to a new country? What family traditions and culture would be accepted in a new place? Does it make a difference if you look different from your friends at school? Most children have experiences in their schools with children who have come from a different culture or racial background, so begin with a classroom sharing of family backgrounds and culture. Bring to the discussion any specific food preferences or traditions that have been carried from one generation to another. Julia is very self-conscious about appearing to be "too Korean." Her mother makes kimchee, a Korean pickled cabbage dish, every day. Consequently, the house always smells like kimchee. Julia's struggle to accept her heritage and become Americanized is one of the themes of this story.

Story Breaks

Story breaks occur wherever the teacher needs to stop for discussion purposes. In this story, breaks should happen to help students recognize any of the elements of resiliency that show how Julia and Patrick deal with the problems associated with raising silkworms. Story breaks will also occur whenever a thematic tie-in occurs. This story lends itself well to discussion of the multiple ways ethnicity and racial perspectives affect the characters' views and behaviors.

Another story break discussion should recognize the multiple perspectives from which the author has chosen to tell the story. For the most part, the story unfolds in the first-person narrative (Julia's point of view), but occasional chapters are devoted to a dialogue between the author and the main character. This perspective allows the reader to gain even more insight into Julia's deepest fears and concerns.

Not all story breaks need to occur for students to comprehend the essence of the tale. Teachers should use their own discretion and consider time and their students' attention abilities before using the story break.

Story Break 1: Julia's Character (Chapters 1–3)

In the first two chapters, the reader will quickly learn that Julia is very sensitive about her Korean background. It is not only the smell of kimchee wafting throughout her house that embarrasses her, but she has also been taunted about her Asian heritage at school. Discussion should focus on how Julia might deal with her ethnic background. Why does Julia prefer a project that seems less Korean and more American? Students should develop an understanding for someone's need to fit in and be just like everyone else. Students may also wish to predict how Patrick will feel if the silkworm project falls through. Why do Patrick's concerns differ from Julia's?

Story Break 2: Author-Character Dialogue (End of Chapter 2)

The author uses an unusual tool to give the reader additional insight into Julia's complex issues. She engages the reader to imagine a discussion between the author and Julia as if the two of them are inventing the story together.

(The discussion appears as a theater script with the different voices represented as parts.) How has the author shown this dialogue in print?

What are Julia's biggest concerns in the telling of her story?

(She wants to make sure Ms. Park, the author, is fair with her character. She is certain she doesn't want her bratty brother to be given too much of the spotlight. Of course, she wants the story to go her way and isn't interested in too many problems.)

How has the author tried to convince Julia that telling a story is more about the truth of feelings rather than the details?

(Ms. Park tells Julia that fiction writing is not necessarily about getting each fact right as much as it is about drawing the character's feelings correctly.)

Story Break 3: Julia's Mom and Racial Prejudice, Strategy 3—Look Within (Chapters 7, 10–12)

Julia and Patrick stay longer than expected at Mr. Dixon's house. Julia's mom becomes enraged with Julia because she had not been informed of the change of plans, but Julia becomes suspicious that her mother's real problem is that she doesn't like Mr. Dixon because he is black. Julia's mother continues to question why Julia and Patrick want to spent so much time with Mr. Dixon. Is her concern that he is black, or is she just wondering why the children want to be spending time with an old man (Chapter 12, p. 154)? The discussion with your students may also refer to Chapter 7 where Julia, Patrick, and her mom first meet Mr. Dixon. Here the discussion may center on who is prejudiced. Just as Julia's mom is uncomfortable with black people, Mr. Dixon is equally surprised to find that Julia and her mom have Asian ancestry.

Julia uses her "Look Within" strategy to cope with her mom's prejudicial feelings and the opinions of Mr. Dixon. When Mr. Dixon innocently refers to her family as Chinese, Julia ponders the meaning of his mistake. In the end, she concludes that not bothering to find out who a person really is, not just the mistaken conclusions someone may draw, would be the real problem.

Story Break 4: Strategy 1—Work on a Talent (All Chapters)

Julia and Patrick have picked a project that no one has ever done. Except for the information they receive from Julia's mother, they must research the project by themselves and address any unforeseen problems by finding the solutions themselves. Throughout the book, students should try to find ways that Patrick and Julia overcome the problems associated with raising silkworms. Do they give up easily, or do they continue to look for answers to the ensuing dilemmas of silkworm farming? In Chapter 13, the children figure out how to film the caterpillars by removing them from their egg carton habitats and slipping them into a glass jar.

Story Break 5: Strategy 3—Look Within; Strategy 4—Rescue Yourself (Chapter 15)

The project is almost a total failure when Julia has second thoughts about killing the worms. After arguing with Patrick and reading the Susan B. Anthony letter (p. 188), Julia finally looks within and finds the solution to her dilemma all by herself. She learns that she can obtain enough thread for the embroidery by killing just five of the cocoons. Julia reasoned that the rest of them would develop into moths and obtain their freedom. In her discovery that there are no perfect solutions to anything, she realizes the importance of finishing the project while maintaining integrity in her own beliefs.

Julia's Tool Box of Resiliency Skills

Julia's Tools	Her Attributes	Student Responses
What she knows	She is intelligent, creative, disciplined, and a hard worker.	
What she has	She has a really special friend, Patrick. She has a great mom (her mom knows how to do embroidery and grow silkworms) and a great dad. She has a friend who owns a mulberry tree.	
What she can do	She can help Patrick learn to care for silkworms. She can learn how to do exquisite embroidery. She can be patient with her mother and her brother, Kenny.	

Using the Tool Box

The teacher may give students the tool box chart as a handout, or it may be created on the whiteboard for display. The student response column may be left blank and filled in by the students as they see how Julia solves her problems. The chart should be designed to help students see how Julia becomes more resilient as she completes the silkworm project.

Vocabulary

Kimchee (p. 1)
Animal husbandry (p. 7)
Maelstrom (p. 32)
Sustainable Farm (p. 131)
Molting (p. 152)
Entomologist (p. 156)
Instar (the stage between moltings; p. 153)
Phobias (p. 157)

Additional Activity: Understanding Sustainability

Mr. Maxwell talks to the children about his sustainable farm. He tells them, "we try to farm here in a way that's good for both the environment and the animals."

Activity One: Building a Sustainable Future

One Well: The Story of Water on Earth by Rochelle Strauss (2007)

How we treat the water on earth will determine our own survival. This book discusses how water is being threatened by our growing populations and our increasing demands for it.

After reading the book to the class, use one of the activities suggested by the author from her Web site: www.kidscanpress.com (click on "Authors and Illustrators" and locate Strauss alphabetically).

Creating a chart to show water use will give students an understanding of how much water is used daily. Class discussion may cover the following questions:

What would happen if we had only half of our daily water supply?

What could you do differently? What could you do without?

Activity Two: Create Waste-Free School Lunches

Modeled after an elementary school in San Rafael, California, students can strive to reduce lunch waste by putting together lunches in package-free containers. Although not as convenient, these lunches tend to be more nutritious. Additionally, children can sort their own trash, recycle, and compost at their school. Children can be encouraged to bring home uneaten food rather than throw it out.

Additional Resources

Ecology Action is a nonprofit organization that works with schools to develop cutting-edge conservation programs. See www.ecoact.org/Programs/programs_schools.htm.

What the Reviewers Said

Library Media Connection (October 2005)

Seventh-graders and best friends/neighbors Julia and Patrick must think of a school project. Patrick is enthusiastic for making silk from silkworms but Julia, who is Korean-American, is afraid the worm project is "too Asian." Julia relents, and first they must find the mulberry leaves that silkworms feed on. After hearing about Mr. Dixon, they go with Julia's mother to ask him if they can have leaves from his tree. When it is revealed that Mr. Dixon is black, Julia's mother's prejudice is obvious. The worms progress through their cycle until Julia is devastated because the pupae must be boiled in order to harvest the silk. Their project comes full-circle, they advance to the state fair, win second place, and their friendship is strengthened. The ups and downs of Julia and Patrick's friendship will hit home for any middle school student. The prejudice issue with Julia's mother is not developed, but lends a twist of irony—Julia is worried about prejudice toward her Korean ethnicity while her mother is displaying prejudice toward African Americans. A unique writing strategy, of two-page dialogue between Julia and the author, is incorporated between each chapter. Through these conversations, the reader finds out more about Julia's character, how and why the author develops the story the way she does, and autobiographical information about Linda Sue Park (she actually has a worm phobia!). Recommended.—Bonnie L. Raasch, Media Specialist, C. B. Vernon Middle School, Marion, Iowa.

Coraline

Neil Gaiman

Story Background: Coraline wanders into an intriguing alternate reality through a mysterious door of her parents' flat where she encounters another mother and father who offer her a more promising future. Appearing quite similar to her own parents, they tempt her with toys and other goodies, drawing Coraline into a confusing web of danger, deception, and mystery.

- Age appropriate for grades 4–8. Highly recommended for Grades 6-8.

- Strategies that develop resiliency: **3—Look Within; 4—Rescue Yourself; 5—Help Others**

Character Study

Coraline—a young girl who likes to explore

Coraline's parents—typical parents who are busy and distracted by their work

The alternate parents—appear to be quite friendly but have a hidden, evil agenda

Miss Spink and Miss Forcible—quirky, friendly old ladies who live in a neighboring flat

Mr. Bobo—an eccentric old man who lives on the top floor

The Cat—seems indifferent to Coraline's situation but eventually becomes an ally

Three lost children—captives of the alternate mother

Introducing This Story to the Class

This decidedly dark tale will fascinate children who enjoy mystery and the creepiness found in horror stories. It is the perfect tale to introduce the element of foreshadowing with its often provocative and compelling descriptions of an eerie mother figure who seems too utterly charming and solicitous to be real. Starting with the cover, students may ponder the kind of story they will read. They should be able to identify the dark colors and the grotesque, shadowy figure as suggestions of foreboding. Looking at the first picture in the book, the teacher might ask what Coraline might encounter once she passes through the door mentioned in the first sentence.

Story Breaks

Story breaks occur wherever the teacher needs to stop for discussion purposes. In this story, breaks should happen to help students recognize any of the elements of foreshadowing that suggest that Coraline will soon be in real danger. Story breaks will also occur whenever Coraline uses one of her resiliency strategies.

Not all story breaks need to occur for students to comprehend the essence of the tale. Teachers should use their own discretion and consider time and their students' attention abilities before using the story break.

Story Break 1: Foreshadowing (Chapter 1, pp. 10–12)

In the first chapter, Coraline is already aware that something is amiss. When she is almost asleep, she is jolted awake by strange sounds and black shadowy things that seem to skitter down the hallway. The author has effectively used the element of foreshadowing to suggest that something eerie will happen beyond the door.

Story Break 2: Foreshadowing (Chapter 2, pp. 20–21)

The two old ladies, Miss Spink and Miss Forcible, offer to read the tea leaves in Coraline's cup. Both women agree that the leaves foretell danger and caution Coraline to be careful. When Miss Spink gives Coraline the stone with a hole in it, the reader will guess that something unfortunate is about to happen.

Story Break 3: Strategy 3—Look Within (Chapter 4, pp. 45–46)

Coraline's first encounter with the other mother reveals that Coraline has intuitive sense and enough self-confidence to reject her offer. Feeling the stone securely in her pocket, Coraline informs the other mother that she is leaving. This scene suggests that Coraline thinks for herself and is not easily swayed by adult suggestions. Coraline reflects on the other mother's offer and knows intuitively that grown-ups can be deceiving.

Story Break 4: Foreshadowing (p. 65)

The cat suggests that the other mother likes games and cannot be trusted.

Story Break 5: Strategy 4—Rescue Yourself

Coraline is the only one that can save herself.

Story Break 6: Strategy 5—Help Others

Coraline decides to save her parents and the other children.

Story Break 7: Foreshadowing (p. 135)

As Coraline flees from the other mother for the last time, it seems she and the cat make it safely home down the dark corridor. What suggests that they are not entirely safe and more trouble may appear soon?

Story Break 8: Foreshadowing

Coraline meets the three children again in her dream. What are they trying to warn her about?

Coraline's Tool Box of Resiliency Skills

Coraline's Tools	Her Attributes	Her Knowledge
What she knows	She likes exploring and is not timid about trying new things.	Her father saved her from wasps, never thinking about his own danger.
What she has	She is brave and enjoys a game, which requires skill. She's been given a stone for protection.	The cat seems to be a friend, and Coraline may need his help. She also has the stone with the hole in it.
What she can do	She can try to find her parents and outwit the other mother in spite of the dangers and risk.	Despite her fears, she will try to save her parents and the other children.

Using the Tool Box

The teacher may give students the tool box chart as a handout, or it may be created on the whiteboard for display. The attributes column may be left blank and filled in by students, or they may write or give their ideas in the third column. The chart should be designed to help students see how Coraline might use her resiliency skills to overcome the other mother.

Vocabulary

haughty
petulantly
splodge
clamber
wraiths
ululating
chitter
beldam

Similes

"Toy tank: . . . lay on the carpet like a beetle on its back." (p. 96)

"It was stuck to the back wall like a slug." (p. 100)

"Cold in the corridor: like stepping down into a cellar on a warm day." (p. 133)

"Sharper than a serpent's tooth is a daughter's ingratitude." (p. 77)

". . . days turn to dust and the leaves fall and the years pass one after the other like the tick-tick-ticking of a clock." (p. 85)

"Something stung her face and hands like sand blowing on a beach on a windy day." (p. 98)

"Pulling the door closed was like trying to close a door against a high wind." (p. 133)

Comprehension Questions

When Coraline returns safely to her home, her parents seem to recall nothing about their imprisonment in the snow globe—did it really happen or not? Why or why not? Give details.

What are the details about the three children that reveal something about their origins and place in time?

What do the eggshell fragments found beneath her pillow mean to Coraline?

What the Reviewers Said

School Library Journal (August 1, 2002)

Gr. 6–8. When Coraline and her parents move into a new house, she notices a mysterious, closed-off door. It originally went to another part of the house, which her family does not own. Some rather eccentric neighbors call her Caroline and seem not to understand her very well, yet they have information for her that will later prove vital. Bored, she investigates the door, which takes her into an alternate reality. There she meets her "other" mother and father. They are very nice to her, which pleases Coraline but also makes her a little suspicious. Her neighbors are in this other world, and they are the same, yet somehow different. When Coraline gets nervous and returns home, her parents are gone. With the help of a talking cat, she figures out that they are being held prisoner by her other parents, as are the souls of some long-lost children. Coraline's plan to rescue them involves, among other things, making a risky bargain with her other mother whose true nature is beginning to show. The rest of the story is a suspense-filled roller coaster, and the horror is all the more frightening for being slightly understated. A droll humor is present in some of the scenes, and the writing is simple yet laden with foreboding. The story is odd, strange, even slightly bizarre, but kids will hang on every word. Coraline is a character with whom they will surely identify, and they will love being frightened out of their shoes. This is just right for all those requests for a scary book.—Bruce Anne Shook, Mendenhall Middle School, Greensboro, NC. Copyright 2002 Cahners Business Information.

A Reading Incentive Program
for the Whole School

The Olympic Reading Challenge

A highly rewarding reading incentive program will extend beyond the classroom-focused resiliency skills and further reinforce the idea that resiliency can be learned through various formats and programs. The following guidelines will allow all students to enjoy reading and sharing regardless of reading levels, age, abilities, or special interests. A successful program not only will encourage students to enjoy reading outside of the classroom but will also involve parents as partners in participation and enthusiasm for the continuous events of the program.

The following program, *The Olympic Reading Challenge,* was implemented for the participation of all students in a suburban K–5 elementary school. Although this program was run by the library staff, any teaching staff, parents, or volunteers would be able to supervise or direct the activities and reward incentives of this program, which required some daily maintenance but minimally affected typical library administrative duties. A student-designed daily news show promoted the program and distributed the rewards and recognition awards; a large chart visible in the library listed the names of all the participants and the number of times each child participated. The following questions may answer some of the most pertinent issues and concerns regarding such a program.

61

Why Create a Reading Incentive Program?

This reading incentive program addressed the concerns of teachers who were looking for ways to reinforce the language and skills of an existing resiliency skills program. Giving rewards and recognition for students who voluntarily chose to read books with the theme of resiliency reinforced the concepts and language taught in the classroom. The sheer number of participants—averaging twenty completed participation sheets per week—showed that as more students participated, others became interested in the program. The program encouraged parents to help their children with either reading or completion of the tasks related to the participation sheets. In this way, the program involved a wide range of talents and reinforcement. Teachers sometimes used the program as an incentive for extra credit grades in the classroom. All in all, this highly visible program was popular with students and created general enthusiasm for books many had not seen before or might have missed altogether.

How Do You Create Interest in a Reading Incentive Program?

Teachers can easily promote the program and its materials with a simple classroom table of books or a special collection display in the library. School announcements or daily news shows give the opportunity to reward students who participate with awards, recognition certificates, or prizes. The school librarian can also make the program both challenging and inventive by changing the displays, adding new books to the resiliency list, and book talking the selections on the resiliency list. Allowing students who have participated to voice their enthusiasm for certain books through book talks or classroom discussion will create added interest in certain titles. A prominently displayed recognition board with bright colors and reward stars or stickers can be the most effective promotional tool of all. Everyone in the school will pass by this board and notice the names and numbers who are participating. No doubt the school librarian—the key person in the program's success—will constantly remind the students to participate by passing out flyers or participation sheets as often as necessary.

How Do I Find Books with Resiliency Themes That Will Address the Reading and Interest Levels of My Students?

The school librarian is the best source for locating specific titles and interests. Included in this book is a listing of current titles available in most libraries with designations for grade-level recommendations under the headings of the specific resiliency strategies cited. In this specific program, the resiliency books were selected and marked with brightly colored dots corresponding to each strategy (1—Work on a Talent, yellow dot; 2—Find a Champion, blue dot, etc.). In this way, students can easily locate a book for the program and identify the strategy addressed.

How Do I Know My Students Are Actually Reading the Books?

This program is designed with accompanying participation sheets for each grade level. Some of the grade levels are combined for ease of use. Forms for K–1 are identical, as are the forms for grades 4 and 5. Each participation sheet asks the student for specifics regarding the resiliency strategy used by the main character. Forms for grades 3–5 ask for specifics as to how the main characters solve their problems. Examples of the forms follow.

Grade 2 – Reading Olympics

Book Title _____   Author _____

1. Work on a Talent   2. Find a Champion   3. Look Inside   4. Rescue Yourself   5. Help Others

Pick one of the "Bounce Back" Strategies above and describe how the character in your story used that way to solve his problem. Circle the number you chose.

Color the dot the same color as the dot on your book.

Red   Yellow   Blue   Green   Pink

Picture by Taia Morley

Your Name: _____

Check the color
dot on your book

○ red

○ yellow

○ blue

○ pink

○ green

Book Title _____

Grade K or 1 (Circle Grade)

Draw a picture to show how your
character never gives up.

Circle the words to show how you would solve the
problem your character had in the story

Help Others

Rescue Yourself

Work on a Talent

Find a Champion

Look Inside

Your Name _____

Picture by Megan Cash

Be a Star—Never Give Up Reading Olympics

Grade 3

Read your book and fill in the form. Your main character (he or she) solves a problem or finds a way to succeed. From the box below, choose one or more of the ways he/she perseveres and bounces back. Explain **how** the character did it. Write at least two sentences with details.

Works on a talent or skill	Finds a champion	Looks within	Rescues herself	Helps others
She discovered that she had a talent or skill.	He finds someone who can help.	He looks at his own strengths. Does he know how to fix it himself or should he ask for help?	She figures out how to solve her own problem.	When things get tough, he looks for ways to help others.

Part One:

_____

_____

_____

Part Two: How would you solve the problem?

_____

_____

_____

Book Title: _____ Author: _____ Your Name: _____

Be a Star—Never Give Up Reading Olympics

Grades 4–5

Read your book and fill in the form. Your main character (he or she) solves a problem or finds a way to succeed. From the box below, choose one or more of the ways he/she perseveres and bounces back. Explain **how** the character did it. Write at least two sentences with details.

Works on a talent or skill	Finds a champion	Looks within	Rescues herself	Helps others
She discovered a talent by working on something she loved to do. By sharpening that skill, her talent became a key to success.	He finds someone who can help with the problem. A teacher, friend, parent or someone else helps out.	He looks at what is available for help. Sometimes there is another meaning in a problem or difficulty that he considers. He looks for new insights to the problem.	She figures out how to solve her own problem. She may even ask for help. She knows how to get help if she needs it.	When things get tough, he looks for ways to help others. Sometimes his own problem seems small when he considers someone else's situation.

_____

_____

_____

_____

_____

_____

_____

Book Title: _____ Author: _____ Your Name: _____

How Long Should a Reading Incentive Program Last?

The length of the program depends on the teachers' goals. It may extend for either a short (six-week program) or long (an entire school year) duration. In this particular program, it ran for the whole school year. The length of the program should be determined by student enthusiasm and interest. If participation seems to be lagging, it may be time to close the program.

Setting up the Program

Once it has been decided that a reading incentive program will be started, information hand-outs should go to teachers, students and parents. A sample memo has been included (Figure 1). Teachers and parents will support the program if they are given adequate information and instruction. Students should also receive information that outlines the program and explains the rules governing their participation. Promotional materials should be gathered and displays planned. Highly visible areas such as hallways, bulletin boards, and display windows should contain relevant information concerning the program. Dates for beginning and ending the program should dovetail with other school events to avoid conflicting schedules. Daily maintenance of the program will be an important component for keeping interest and participation at high levels. Staff should be assigned duties that must be maintained on a regular basis such as record keeping and consistent distribution of prizes. If the program involves the whole school, events and outcomes should be reported on a regular basis.

Teacher Memo

Olympic Reading Challenge

The library will begin a new reading incentive program titled the Olympic Reading Challenge. This program will feature a list of books with resiliency themes to complement the school's character education program. From this list, kids will read a variety of books and submit to the library a form for each completed book. This reading incentive program will use the Olympics ("Be a Star," "Never Give Up") as its theme, and any child who reads five books (one from each strategy for resiliency) will receive a patch from the library. The patches are attractive colors in multiple designs and may be sewn on a backpack or clothing. In May, the library will have a final contest for all those who qualify (that is, who read at least five books), and they may submit an essay. We will then choose at least five winners who will receive gold medals with blue ribbon necklaces. This program will be something accessible to all grade levels and will be implemented in a way so that all can participate.

Figure 1. Teacher Memo

Finalizing the Program

Ideally, the program will end with an event that rewards those students who have shown the greatest enthusiasm and consistently participated throughout the school year. This reading incentive program, titled the Olympic Reading Challenge, ended with the top five participants receiving imitation Olympic gold medals with blue ribbons in a special ceremony on the school news show. Rewarding the class or the grade level that had the most participants are other possibilities for recognition. The important thing is that there be some kind of recognition that publicly honors the accomplishments of the participants and instills a sense of pride in regard to their voluntary achievements.

Following are sample entry forms for the essay contest for grades K–2 and 3–5.

Olympic Gold Medal Entry Form: Grades K–2

Here's what to do: Recall one of the five books you read for the Olympic Reading Challenge (ORC). Write the title below.

_____

Your Name:_____

All the books in the ORC have the theme of "Resiliency." That means how you "bounce back" whenever you are disappointed, discouraged, or feel sad or mad. In each story, the main character never gives up and finally finds a way out. Write a short essay that tells what you learned from this character. What do you admire most about this character and how she/he did it? Be sure to give an example. What would you do if you were faced with the same problem? How would you solve the problem? Draw a picture on a blank page.

How Your Essay Will Be Scored

Points _____

20	Explaining what you learned from this character
20	Showing an example of how the character solved the problem
20	Explaining how you admire this character
20	Telling how you would solve this problem
20	Drawing a picture that shows what happened

Please note:

Child may tell the essay and parents may write the sentences for those in grades K–1.

Olympic Gold Medal Entry Form: Grades 3–5

Here's what to do: Recall one of the five books you read for the Olympic Reading Challenge (ORC). Write the title below.

_____

Your Name:_____

All the books in the ORC have the theme of "Resiliency." That means how you "bounce back" whenever you are disappointed, discouraged, or feel sad or mad. In each story the main character uses one or more strategies to solve his/her problem. Those strategies are as follows:

Works on a Talent or Skill	Finds a Champion	Looks Within	Rescues Self	Helps Others
She discovered a talent by working on something she loved to do. By sharpening that skill, her talent became a key to success.	He finds someone who can help with the problem. A teacher, friend, parent or someone else helps out.	He looks at what is available for help. Sometimes there is another meaning in a problem or difficulty that he considers. He looks for new insights to the problem.	She figures out how to solve her own problem. She may even ask for help. She knows how to get help if she needs it.	When things get tough, he looks for ways to help others. Sometimes his own problem seems small when he considers someone else's situation.

On a separate piece of paper, write a one-page essay about how you would solve any problem or difficult situation and use one or more of the strategies listed above. Be sure to use an example from one of the books to tell how you could relate your personal ability to solve the problem to the strategy used by that character. Attach the essay to this form.

How Your Essay Will Be Scored

Points _____

20	You remembered to use one of the strategies
20	You related your strategy to one of the character's strategies
20	You used a specific example from one of the books
20	You wrote in complete sentences and used standard grammar
20	You supported the points you made with adequate details

Your final essay should be attached to this form.

From *Bounce Back!: Resiliency Strategies Through Children's Literature* by Mary Humphrey. Westport, CT: Libraries Unlimited. Copyright © 2008.

Olympic Reading Challenge

Read five books from the Olympic Reading Challenge list and qualify to receive a Gold Medal in June. You have about five months to read one book from each of the five colors, red, blue, yellow, green and pink. You'll find the books displayed in the library in designated areas.

After you read one of the books, designated by a colored dot on the spine, you may request a form from Mrs. _____. Follow the directions on the form and bring it to the library during your library class. Once we receive the form, you will get:

A Certificate for Participation (first book)

A bookmark (for every book after the first)

A stamp on our Olympic Display at the library

After you have read five books, you will receive the patch of your choice (which may be sewn on your backpack or clothing), and you qualify for the Gold Medal Challenge in June.

Grades 4–5: must read at least three chapter books

Grade 3: must read at least two chapter books

Grades K–2: may read any of the books

Frequently asked questions:

May a parent read the book to you? Yes

May you listen to the book on tape or CD if that format is available? Yes

Literacy Suggestions Supporting the Concept of Resiliency

Picture Books and Middle Grade Fiction That Demonstrate the Five Strategies

These five strategies are helpful guides in the development of resiliency:

(1) Work on a Talent, (2) Find a Champion, (3) Look Within, (4) Rescue Yourself, (5) Help Others

The annotations for the books on this list are reproduced with the permission of Follett Library Resources, Inc. Copyright 2008. All rights reserved.

Grade Levels	Strategies	Library Call Number	Title	Description
2–5	1, 4, 5	738 AND	*The Pot That Juan Built* by Nancy Andrews-Goebel; pictures by David Diaz. Lee & Low Books, 2002.	A cumulative rhyme summarizes the life's work of renowned Mexican potter, Juan Quezada. Additional information describes the process he uses to create his pots after the style of the Casas Grandes people.
2–4	1	E ALI	*Marianthe's Story. One: Painted Words; Marianthe's Story. Two: Spoken Memories* by Aliki. Greenwillow Books, 1998.	Title from separate title pages; works issued back-to-back and inverted. Two separate stories, the first telling of Mari's starting school in a new land and the second describing village life in her country before she and her family left in search of a better life.
3–5	4	E ARN	*The Pumpkin Runner* by Marsha Diane Arnold; pictures by Brad Sneed. Dial Books for Young Readers, 1998.	An Australian sheep rancher who eats pumpkins for energy enters a race from Melbourne to Sydney, despite people laughing at his eccentricities.
3–5	1, 5	E BAR	*Radio Rescue* by Lynne Barasch. Farrar, Straus & Giroux, 2000.	In 1923, after learning Morse code and setting up his own amateur radio station, a twelve-year-old boy sends a message that leads to the rescue of a family stranded by a hurricane in Florida. Based on experiences of the author's father.

Grade Levels	Strategies	Library Call Number	Title	Description
K–3	1, 3, 4, 5	E BUE	*Superdog: The Heart of a Hero* by Caralyn Buehner; illustrated by Mark Buehner. HarperCollins, 2004.	Tired of being overlooked because he is so small, a big-hearted dog named Dexter transforms himself into a superhero.
K–2	3, 4	E COC	*Bravery Soup* by Maryann Cocca-Leffler. Albert Whitman, 2005.	Big Bear offers fearful Carlin the raccoon some of his Bravery Soup in return for collecting a secret ingredient for it. Carlin, of course, overcomes his fears while retrieving the ingredient and is rewarded with Bear's soup, served only "to the brave."
K–2	1, 4	E FOX	*Koala Lou* by Mem Fox; illustrated by Pamela Lofts. Harcourt Brace, 1988.	A young koala, longing to hear her mother speak lovingly to her as she did before other children came along, plans to win her distracted parent's attention.
1–3	1, 3, 4	E FUN	*The Princess Knight* by Cornelia Funke; illustrations by Kerstin Meyer; translated by Anthea Bell. Chicken House/Scholastic, 2004 (2001).	Princess Violetta, raised by her widowed father, the king, to ride and joust just like her brothers, is horrified when he announces plans to hold a tournament in which the winner will gain her hand in marriage.
K–2	3	E HEN	*Lilly's Purple Plastic Purse* by Kevin Henkes.	Lilly loves everything about school, especially her teacher, but when he asks her to wait a while before showing the class her new purse, she does something for which she is very sorry later.

Grade Levels	Strategies	Library Call Number	Title	Description
2–4	2, 5	E JOH	*Amber on the Mountain* by Tony Johnston; paintings by Robert Duncan. Puffin Books, 1998 (1994).	Isolated on her mountain, Amber meets and befriends a girl from the city who gives her the determination to learn to read and write.
2–4	1, 2, 4, 5	E MAR	*The Raft* by Jim LaMarche. HarperCollins, 2000.	Reluctant Nicky spends a wonderful summer with Grandma who introduces him to the joy of rafting down the river near her home and watching the animals along the banks.
3–5	1, 2, 4, 5	E MAY	*Shibumi and the Kitemaker*, story and pictures by Mercer Mayer. Marshall Cavendish, 1999.	After seeing the disparity between the conditions of her father's palace and the city beyond its walls, the emperor's daughter has the royal kitemaker build a huge kite to take her away from it all.
3–5	1, 5	E MCC	*Mirette on the High Wire* by Emily Arnold McCully. Putnam & Grosset, 1992.	Mirette learns tightrope walking from Monsieur Bellini, a guest in her mother's boarding house, not knowing that he is a celebrated tightrope artist who has withdrawn from performing because of fear.
2–5	2, 3, 4	E MCK	*Goin' Someplace Special* by Patricia C. McKissack; illustrated by Jerry Pinkney. Atheneum Books for Young Readers, 2001.	In segregated 1950s Nashville, a young African American girl braves a series of indignities and obstacles to get to one of the few integrated places in town: the public library.
3–5	2, 3	E MIL	*Secret of the Peaceful Warrior: A Story about Courage and Love* by Dan Millman; illustrated by T. Taylor Bruce. H.J. Kramer, 1991.	An old man named Socrates shows Danny that the best way of dealing with a bully is the way of the peaceful warrior, through courage and love.

Grade Levels	Strategies	Library Call Number	Title	Description
2–4	1, 2, 4	E MOR	*Tomas and the Library Lady* by Pat Mora; illustrated by Raul Colon. Knopf, distributed by Random House, 1997.	While helping his family in their work as migrant laborers far from their home, Tomas finds an entire world to explore in the books at the local public library.
K–3	1, 3, 5	E MOR	*Wombat Goes Walkabout* by Michael Morpurgo. Candlewick Press, 2000.	While looking for his mother, wombat meets many animals that are not impressed with his talent for digging, but when a fire approaches, they change their minds.
K–2	3	E PAR	*It's Okay to Be Different* by Todd Parr. Little, Brown, 2001.	Illustrations and brief text describe all kinds of differences that are "okay," such as being a different color, needing some help, being adopted, and having a different nose.
3–5	2, 3, 5	E POL	*Thank You, Mr. Falker* by Patricia Polacco. Philomel Books, 1998.	At first, Trisha loves school, but her difficulty learning to read makes her feel dumb until, in the fifth grade, a new teacher helps her understand and overcome her problem.
2–5	3, 4, 5	E POL	*Appelemando's Dreams* by Patricia Polacco. Philomel, 1991.	Because he spends his time dreaming, the villagers are convinced that Appelemando will never amount to much. But in time, his dreams change the village, and all the people in it.
K–3	1, 4	E PUL	*Axle Annie* by Robin Pulver; pictures by Tedd Arnold. Puffin, 2001 (1999).	The schools in Burskyville never close for snow because Axle Annie is always able to make it up the steepest hill in town, until Shifty Rhodes and Hale Snow set out to stop her.

Grade Levels	Strategies	Library Call Number	Title	Description
1–3	4, 5	E RAY	*Mr. and Mrs. Pig's Evening Out* by Mary Rayner. Atheneum, 1976.	Mr. and Mrs. Pig's new babysitter is not what she seems, but their ten piglets prove masters of the situation.
3–5	1, 4, 5	E WIL	*Library Lil* by Suzanne Williams; illustrated by Steven Kellogg. Puffin Books, 2001 (1997).	A formidable librarian makes readers out of not only the once-resistant residents of her small town but a tough-talking, television-watching motorcycle gang as well.
4–5	1, 4, 5	F CLE	*A Week in the Woods* by Andrew Clements. Simon & Schuster Books for Young Readers, 2002.	The fifth grade's annual camping trip in the woods tests Mark's survival skills and his ability to relate to a teacher who seems out to get him.
4–5	1, 2, 3	F COD	*Sahara Special* by Esme Raji Codell. Hyperion Books For Children, 2003.	Struggling with school and her feelings since her father left, Sahara gets a fresh start with a new and unique teacher who supports her writing talents and the individuality of each of her classmates.
4–5	2, 3, 4	F CRE	*Ruby Holler* by Sharon Creech. Joanna Cotler Books, 2002.	Thirteen-year-old fraternal twins Dallas and Florida have grown up in a terrible orphanage but their lives change forever when an eccentric but sweet older couple invites them each on an adventure, beginning in an almost magical place called Ruby Holler.
4–5	1, 2, 3, 4	F CUR	*Bud, Not Buddy* by Christopher Paul Curtis. Delacorte Press, 1999.	Ten-year-old Bud, a motherless boy living in Flint, Michigan, during the Great Depression, escapes a bad foster home and sets out in search of the man he believes to be his father—the renowned bandleader H. E. Calloway of Grand Rapids.

Grade Levels	Strategies	Library Call Number	Title	Description
4–5	1, 4, 5	F DIC	*The Tale of Despereaux: Being the Story of a Mouse, a Princess, Some Soup, and a Spool of Thread* by Kate DiCamillo; illustrated by Timothy Basil Ering. Candlewick Press, 2003.	The adventures of Despereaux Tilling, a small mouse of unusual talents, the princess whom he loves, the servant girl who longs to be a princess, and a devious rat determined to bring them all to ruin.
4–5	3, 4, 5	F HIA	*Hoot* by Carl Hiaasen. Alfred A. Knopf, distributed by Random House, 2002.	Roy, who is new to his small Florida community, becomes involved in another boy's attempt to save a colony of burrowing owls from a proposed construction site.
4–5	3, 4, 5	F IBB	*The Star of Kazan* by Eva Ibbotson; illustrated by Kevin Hawkes. Dutton Children's Books, 2004.	Annika, a twelve-year-old foundling in late-nineteenth-century Vienna, inherits a trunk of costume jewelry, and soon afterward a woman claiming to be her aristocratic mother arrives and takes her to live in a strangely decrepit mansion in Germany.
2–5	1, 3, 4	F JOR	*Salt in His Shoes: Michael Jordan in Pursuit of a Dream* by Deloris Jordan with Roslyn M. Jordan; illustrated by Kadir Nelson. Simon & Schuster, 2000.	A young Michael Jordan puts salt in his shoes, hoping it will help him grow tall enough to become a famous basketball player.

Grade Levels	Strategies	Library Call Number	Title	Description
3–5	2	F MIL	*Richard Wright and the Library Card* by William Miller; illustrated by Gregory Christie. Lee & Low Books, 1997.	Based on a scene from Wright's autobiography, *Black Boy*, in which the seventeen-year-old African American borrows a white man's library card and devours every book as a ticket to freedom.
4–5	3, 4, 5	F PRA	*The Wee Free Men* by Terry Pratchett. HarperCollins, 2003.	Tiffany, a young witch-to-be in the land of Discworld, teams up with the Wee Free Men, a clan of six-inch-high blue toughs, to rescue her baby brother and ward off a sinister invasion from Fairyland.

Credits and Acknowledgments

The author and publisher gratefully acknowledge permission to use excerpts from the following material:

"Look Within" and "Work on a Talent" illustrations are by Megan Montague Cash.

"Find a Champion," "Help Others," and "Rescue Yourself" illustrations by Taia Morley.

The annotations for the Literacy Suggestions list are reproduced with the permission of Follett Library Resources, Inc. Copyright © 2008. All rights reserved.

Landed review (p. 16) reprinted by permission from *Library Media Connection*, Volume 25, Issue 3, Copyright © 2006 by Linworth Publishing, Inc. All rights reserved.

The Librarian of Basra review (p. 22) reprinted by permission from Library Media Connection, Volume 24, Issue 1, Copyright © 2005 by Linworth Publishing, Inc. All rights reserved.

The Scarecrow and His Servant review (p. 46) reprinted by permission from *Library Media Connection*, Volume 24, Issue 5, Copyright © 2006 by Linworth Publishing, Inc. All rights reserved.

Project Mulberry review (p. 56) reprinted by permission from *Library Media Connection*, Volume 24, Issue 2, Copyright © 2005 by Linworth Publishing, Inc. All rights reserved.

Index

About the Author

MARY HUMPHREY is a previous Libraries Unlimited author. She is currently teacher librarian for the West Genesee Central School District near Syracuse, New York.